THE
ESSENTIAL
REBECCA
WEST

UNCOLLECTED PROSE

Published by Pearhouse Press, Inc., Pittsburgh, PA 15208
www.pearhousepress.com

First North American Printing: May 2010

Printed in the United States of America

Library of Congress Control Number: 2009937193

ISBN: 978-0-9802355-5-5

Cover and Book Design: Mike Murray

THE ESSENTIAL REBECCA WEST

UNCOLLECTED PROSE

PEARHOUSE
PRESS

Acknowledgements

As the co-executor of the literary estate of Rebecca West, I would like to give profound thanks for help with compiling this collection, which involved an exciting adventure in literary archaeology. In the summer of 2007, Rebecca West scholars Bernard Schweizer, Ann Norton and Debra Rae Cohen came with me on a trip to Tulsa, Oklahoma to dig through the archives at the McFarlin Special Collections at the University of Tulsa. We wanted to plunder the vast archive of Rebecca's writings that had either never been published at all, or had been published only once, in a newspaper or magazine, decades ago—usually well outside the scope of any Web-based archive. There were two reasons for wanting to do this. First, there is the value of making good work by dead writers widely available—it keeps living authors on their toes, if nothing else, and feeds the scholar's hunger for more material. Second, and more importantly, we wanted there to be something to offer the reader who is merely curious about Rebecca, has heard her name mentioned and wants to know more, but is unsure where to start and is understandably daunted by the prospect of picking up a 500,000 word book about Yugoslavia in the 1930s. We weren't sure what we would find. As you will see, we made out like Indiana Jones.

Bernard, Ann and Debra Rae then worked tirelessly with me over many months to sift, type up, edit and finally choose the collection you now hold in your hands.

Long Island University donated money towards our stay in Tulsa, which helped make it possible, and we thank them, too.

Further, the staff at the McFarlin Special Collections were incredibly helpful and generally tolerant of the disruptive explosions of surprise, delight and laughter that marked our progress through this treasure trove of Rebecca's writings.

Lastly, I would like to thank Rebecca's biographer, Carl Rollyson, who has always been ready to lend a helping hand with information, comment and encouragement.

— *Helen Macleod Atkinson, May 2010*

TABLE OF CONTENTS

THE ESSENTIAL REBECCA WEST

INTRODUCTION

by Anne Bobby

T he greatest writer you've never heard of...' You hear that a lot about Rebecca West. She's not like other notable authors of her time, writers like Ayn Rand, or C. S. Lewis, or Virginia Woolf, or even her lover, H. G. Wells. These are names you know, whose titles you recognize and may have possibly read (or at least, if you're like me, read in part). These are writers you know were great, and that affords them your respect, if not necessarily your passion for their writings.

Yet readers of Rebecca West hang her portrait in their offices and quote her with abandon. They set out to read everything she's written (including *Black Lamb and Grey Falcon*, the paperback of which comes in at nearly twelve-hundred pages), and applaud the long-overdue release of a book like this collection. Readers of Rebecca West are committed, like disciples, to making hers a household name, or at least elevating her works to a recognition long overdue. She's high priestess of a literary cult, for when you're bit by Rebecca, you are well and truly *bit*.

I was among the uninitiated until 2004, when I had the opportunity to portray her in a one-woman show that I co-wrote with Helen Atkinson and Carl Rollyson. During that Off-Broadway run (and the subsequent productions in Amsterdam and the Hague), she began to take hold of me, and I realized how ill-suited the phrase 'one-woman' applied to anything to do with Cicely Fairfield, a woman of such diverse interests and fearless artistry it seems as if she emerged into the literary world as not one Rebecca West, but a dozen.

Perhaps this is the reason so many people who should know, indeed devour, the writings of Rebecca have never sought out her works. You don't find more than a volume or two of hers on any one subject anywhere. Instead, you find her writings spanned most topics and, until recently, have remained scattered about the literary universe. She is a challenge to explore, for she is so very challenging to classify.

Rebecca West wasn't a feminist writer, or journalist, or critic, or essayist, or author, but all of these; she wrote neither fiction nor nonfiction, neither reviews nor travelogues, but all of them. She wore every hat and crossed every genre—sometimes all at once.

I remember a line from the play in which Rebecca, traveling in Mexico with her husband, Henry, visits Trotsky's grave, and in speaking with his grandson feels the idea for what would have been her last book, her "final algebra of human suffering," take shape:

"I would tell (Trotsky's) story, and mixed into it...would be my marriage, my family background and Henry's, the Aztecs, Meso-American art, the Spanish conquest, Cortes and Montezuma, even Napoleon. For we were all exiles and survivors...Though it was a huge pyramid of a book to scale, I hardly noticed."

Only Rebecca West could have written a book like that, and made it not only coherent, but utterly riveting.

Yet it wasn't just her supreme intellect and curiosity that makes her so fascinating to those in the know. What makes her works resonate—what adds luster to her thoughts and buffs them to a high shine of wit and clarity, and what has been lost to the uninitiated, is her *essence*. Readers knew Rebecca West and read her columns and reviews faithfully, laying down money for the *New York Times*, *The Telegraph*—any publication that ran her pieces. There was a reason that *Time* magazine called her 'indisputably the world's number one woman writer' in 1947—she was *read*. Everywhere.

Today, we have the opportunity to know even more about her, and add a new patina to works we may already know. We read her essays on the Nuremburg trials knowing that Harold Ross tapped her for the job because she would be unswayed by Goering's attempts at intimidation. No doubt her fellow journalists concurred, and her readers were captivated. But how many people could have dreamed at the time that while sending on her searing dispatches she conducted an affair with one of the chief prosecutors? No wonder Goering didn't stand a chance against her.

We have greater insight to her struggles as well as her triumphs. We read her essays on feminism and family life knowing not just of her early devotion to the suffrage (her first thoughts on the subject were published at fourteen), but also of her yearnings for a father who deserted her as a child, and the difficulties she faced as an unwed mother, the result of long and clandestine love affair with H. G. Wells. We know as well of the acrimonious relationship with the son born of that union, and the book he would write about her which severed their relationship. To her peers and her readers, she was known as a firebrand—only now do we have a fuller understanding of that fire's source.

We can learn so much about her, and from her. I can't imagine any reader reading these essays and not coming away with a new way of regarding history as it's been taught, as well as history as it unfolds, and regarding their world with fresh eyes—eyes that embrace and repel, concede and confront and pull from the farthest reaches of humanity cohesive and dazzling perspective.

She played by rules even as she played *with* them, and that is why we celebrate her. She is not so much a product of her age as she is a *counter*-product—and the perfect foil for our time.

What a great lady to know.

— *Brooklyn, 2010*

THE ESSENTIAL REBECCA WEST

Essays

ENCOUNTER

From the INTERNATIONAL LITERARY ANNUAL, *1959*

L ong ago, one autumn night in the twenties, I went to a party in New York which was given by a film magnate named Mike. I had been to the opera and arrived late, at the same time as an elderly foreigner who was a stranger to me, whose name I did not hear when we were introduced and whose features I cannot recall. I gathered nothing about him except that he was a person of consequence, and I gathered this only because my host finished the introduction by waving his clasped hands over his head, as if he were the second of a victorious boxer. The foreigner was obviously puzzled by this gesture and began to enquire what it meant, but either did not know enough English for even that or was too tired, and perhaps too irritated to trouble. I would have tried to speak French with him, although I thought he was either Italian or Spanish, had I not just been greeted by a man I had known for some years, who was a famous film star. He had brought with him one of the most beautiful girls I have ever seen, a tall and slender creature with bobbed golden hair and a long neck, who wore a dress of pale gold silk dripping with crystal beads and barely covering her exquisite knees, according to the fashion of those days, which is even now being revived. She looked like a yellow tulip with a very long stalk, and she had the further advantage of a singularly friendly smile, empty of the pride she might reasonably have felt.

It was a crowded party, and the four of us, the foreigner and the film star and his girl-friend and myself, were hemmed in together between a suit of armour and a large group of wooden life-sized figures representing the Marriage at Cana, a work in the tradition of Tilman Riemenschneider. These figures the foreigner contemplated with a factitious absorption; he plainly did not want anyone to speak to him. The film star questioned me about London friends, and the beautiful girl took a caviar sandwich offered by a footman, and told me with an air of shrewd discovery that she thought it a good thing to eat when one was hungry. Presently another footman brought us a salver laden with glasses of champagne. The beautiful girl said that she did not use hard liquor, nor coffee neither, because she had been raised as a Seventh Day Adventist. But the rest of us each took a glass. The film star was the first to taste his drink, and then he leaned towards me and said tensely, "Your horse is pregnant."

I was astonished. I had no horse and I could not see how, even if I had had one, the film star would have become aware of its state of health. I repeated quite loudly, wanting to get the thing clear, "My horse is pregnant?" I was again astonished. A look of horror passed over the film star's face, and he whispered, "For crying out loud, Mike is just behind you." But why, if a horse, mine or anyone else's, was pregnant, should it be kept from Mike? In fact, the phrase was one current in those days when Prohibition was still in force, and it was useful to have a few words that could be muttered under one's breath at any party where the drinks seemed dangerous. It is a tag-line from an unpleasing story about an analytical chemist. There can rarely have been a more appropriate occasion for using it than that party. I can remember the taste of that champagne now. It was like a mixture of golden syrup and vinegar, and it had a curious greasy quality, as if some mayonnaise had been stirred into it; its fizziness seemed the result of its own indigestion. The film star and I went on holding our glasses but drank no more. To our surprise the foreigner emptied his glass and had another one, which seemed an odd action for a man whose home was almost certainly in some wine-drinking country. As he drank he kept his eyes fixed, in the melancholy abstraction which is almost all I can remember of him, on the group representing the Marriage at Cana, perhaps in hope.

Our group broke up and we found other friends, but when I found myself in the hall, ready to go home, I met the film star and his girl-friend again. He offered to drive me to my hotel, and we three went out into a street that was as brilliant as the house we had just left, though New York was ill lit in those days. There was a huge moon rolling across the sky, and the pavement was snow-white, and the shadows of the houses were soot-black. The Japanese chauffeur helped us in and we were just about to start when the host came out of the house with the elderly foreigner and asked the film star if he would mind dropping him at his hotel on Park Avenue. Again Mike's gesture indicated that the foreigner was a person of consequence; after he had helped him into the car he pointed at him and then clapped his hands and nodded and beamed, as if he were applauding in a theatre or a concert-hall. After we drove off he remained on the sidewalk, clapping away. The foreigner sank low in his seat between the beautiful girl and myself, as if fleeing from any further view of his host, and uttered a low moan of exasperation. He yawned several times and moved uneasily, stammered a few words of thanks for our kindness in taking him home, then yawned again.

It was quite apparent that he was suffering from indigestion, and no wonder, since he had had two glasses of that champagne. The beautiful girl, who was much taller than he was, leaned over him in sudden tenderness and said, "Alka-Seltzer." He looked puzzled and she repeated it sweetly, helpfully, "Alka-Seltzer." His features twitched irritably, as if more were being asked of him than he could give, and closed his eyes. I suppose that if one did not know the meaning of the word "Alka-Seltzer," and a beautiful girl murmured it to one, bending her beauty towards one, one might get a wrong impression. But we thought no more about him, because just then the car went into Central Park, which was flooded with moonlight, a dazzling silver enclosure in the middle of the black and white town. "Drive slowly," said the film star, and when we got to the lake the beautiful girl said,

"Oh, can't we stop a mite?" and we did.

"I would like to get out and walk for a minute," I said and the others sighed ecstatically and agreed. The foreigner was now really asleep and had tilted towards me, for no other reason, I am sure, than that it was not I who had murmured the disturbing word to him. We propped him up and got out of the car, and were at once lapped in a pure loveliness not often seen except among snowfields or in the air above the clouds. The lake in Central Park is curiously unspoiled. It looks very much as it must have done when the Indians owned Manhattan Island, with trees and bushes growing from rocks and boulders as if this were a clearing in a forest and not in a city. It is always agreeable, and at this moment it was uplifting, it held the essence of the untarnished night. We could look round us at the tall buildings on the edges of the park, where the darkness was diluted by the flush which hangs above the city lights; but here we enjoyed night in its full intensity. Above us the moon and the stars shone against a sky that was nearly black. Round the lake the Fenimore Cooper pattern of rocks and trees was strongly drawn in moonlight and shadow, and the water itself was the brightest silver I have ever seen, giving back to the moon brighter than it got.

I said, "How lovely it would be to be on the lake in a boat." Rarely have I ever wanted to do that. It seemed as if this little basin of water had a special connection with the moon, was at the end of a miraculous ladder of light.

The film star pointed out that there was a boathouse at the end of the lake and that probably there would be boats inside. I said that there were, I sometimes rowed there in the mornings, but that it would be locked. To this he answered that his Japanese boy could open anything in the world. (On reflection this seems to me one of the oddest parts of this story. Would you like to employ a chauffeur who had acquired the art of opening anything?) I pointed out that even if the Japanese boy got into the boathouse a policeman or park-keeper was bound to appear and to disapprove. The film star explained that there were no policemen or park-keepers in Central Park at night, that was why people got held up and robbed all the time. He would not be standing there with us two girls if the Japanese boy had not two guns with him, one down by the wheel, one up in a holster slung from the roof of the car, in case he was made to put up his hands. At that the beautiful girl sighed, "you're wunnerful," and the thing was as good as done. Nor did I really try to raise a dissuading voice. I wanted so much to be on that silver core of this black and white world. And indeed I thought it possible that the film star was right and Central Park was left unguarded at night. It is a place where strange things happen. Once some resourceful people, learning that the drug marijuana can be raised from a particular kind of birdseed, planted some in one of the Central Park flower-beds, nursed it to maturity and harvested the crop at great profit, and repeated the feat for several seasons before they were detected.

Very soon a dark shape nosed out of the boathouse and very soon we were all out on the silver water, and it was as good as I had thought it would be. We all stared at the moon. The film star said that he wished he could get a script that had this in it. He flung out his arm in a gesture of artistic frustration. The beautiful girl said that she wished she could be a hospital nurse; she was, it appeared, in some form of musical show that had succeeded the Ziegfeld Follies. Then we all fell silent. The beautiful girl and I threw off our cloaks, though it was not too warm, as if moon-bathing had the same sort of virtue as sun-bathing. I felt a milder, but still strong, form of the pleasure that is to be got by swimming in a cold sea. But there was more to the moment than a sense of physical well-being. Peace poured down on us; in the pure light life was undefiled. I was intensely happy for about five minutes, and then there came a roar from the bank. For of course there were policemen in Central Park at night, and we must have been very visible in that boat. Like the beautiful girl, I was wearing a dress dripping with crystal beads, and we must have shone in the moonlight like two chandeliers.

There were two policemen, one Irish and one Jewish; and one of them had a motorcycle. Both would, I think, have taken the matter calmly had it not been for errors that two of my companions were forced by their temperaments to make. The Irish policeman expressed the opinion as, at his urgent behest we got out of the boat, that we must all be well liquored up to be doing a fool thing like this; and that is what all his experience had led him to believe. Only people who were drunk would want to break into a boathouse in order to drift about on a lake, in not very warm weather, at something like two in the morning, and he and his colleague would have pardoned us if we had indeed been drunk, and had therefore fitted into the pattern of the universe as they recognised it. But the beautiful girl was compelled by her amiability and candour, which made her anxious to give correct information to those likely to be interested in it, to state, as she had done when offered champagne at the party, that she did not use hard liquor, nor coffee neither, on account of having been raised a Seventh Day Adventist.

The policemen felt she was laughing at them, and one said sourly that she didn't look no Seventh Day Adventist to him. She was also drawing attention to our absurd, our inconsistent sobriety. Coldly they walked us down to the boathouse, and there the second error was committed. It would have been useless for the Japanese chauffeur to have denied that he had picked the padlock on the door with the steel wire he was holding in his hand, but his desire to please made him bow and smile and claim that he had done no damage to the lock—"easy job," he said, several times, "for me—very easy job"—and furthermore, that he would be able to leave it exactly as he had found it. There it was. We were stone cold sober, and we were accompanied by what appeared to be an experienced burglar. They told us to follow the motorcycle to the nearest police-station.

When we returned to the car I was relieved to find that the foreigner was still asleep, but it seemed to me that it might be a shock to him if he suddenly woke up and found that he was being conveyed to a police-station. When I said this to my companions they did not quite understand what I meant. The beautiful girl said that if he was travelling in the United States it would be interesting (she left out the middle t) for him to see how the police worked. The film star said that he would be all right, do him good, and there wasn't going to be any trouble, this wasn't taxes or a money charge, and he knew the Mayor of New York and the Police Commissioner. We would just go to the station to oblige these two boys and get it over. "I've been wunner-ing why you didn't tell them who you are," said the beautiful girl. "I think they're ignorant," said the film star. "Better save it up for who's in charge of the station." They were unapprehensive and were getting sleepy. The beautiful girl yawned and stretched, and curled up in her corner; the film star's chin sank to his shirt-front, the foreigner's head bobbed against my shoulder. I was alone with my fears, which were not acute, I had really so much enjoyed my five minutes in the boat.

The film star had been right about the advisability of saving it up for the man in charge of the station. He was a fat and laughing know-all who looked up as the film star came in, and called him by his name.[1] The film star produced a cigar case and handed it round while he explained that it was all his own fault, he had run into trouble with these two good conscientious boys in Central Park, and he had gladly come along to straighten things out. Beside him the beautiful girl stood in her glittering dress, tall and leggy like a crane, rubbing her eyes under the fierce light of the electric light bulbs under their enamel shades. I was frightened, as all Europeans are, by the sordid interior decoration favoured by the law when it settles down to the disagreeable side of its work, by those harsh lights, the chocolate paint that went half-way up the walls, the smell of the disinfectant floor-wash. The film star went on to recount how these two kids had taken a fancy to go on the lake, and he had wanted to give them what they wanted; and he pretended to recall that he had broken into that same boathouse when he was a boy on Eleventh Street, and he hoped he would never forget those days, and so he had got his Japanese boy to do what he had done, just for the hell of it. I could not have justly been called a kid at that time, I was about thirty, but I did not avert my face from the light, for I rather suspected that the film star was representing himself as a nice guy who treated a woman as if she were younger than she was, and I was anxious that whatever game he was playing should succeed.

It succeeded. The Irish and the Jewish policemen had realised they were beaten from the moment the sergeant had greeted the film star with such a cordial waggle of all his chins, and they went off with their cigars, glad to get that much out of the affair. But we had to buy ourselves out of the station with talk. The sergeant was the kind of man who reads the gossip columns. He knew all about the film star's films and the affairs of the studio which employed him; he knew the principals and the management of the beautiful girl's show; he knew the owner and the editor of the newspaper for which I was working. We had to tell him things about all these people, but he could never wait till any of us finished a story, he had to get on to another; we found ourselves engaged on a task as dreary as saying "Yes," to names read out of the telephone directory. He meant no harm, and in time we were showed a courtesy not likely to be enjoyed by any person taken to a London police-station in the middle of the night on the charge of, say, breaking into the bathing pavilion on the Serpentine.

We were all of us, including the Japanese chauffeur, taken away and given a meal of ham and eggs and coffee and doughnuts, shared by the sergeant and two other policemen. I think this meal must have been served not in the police-station but in a small restaurant next door, for I remember a lot of holy pictures on the wall and some flowers in a holder shaped like a gnome in front of a plaster statue of the Madonna. The beautiful girl ate heartily, but as the coffee pot went round she told us again that she was a Seventh Day Adventist, and never used it; and one of the policemen said that it was a very good religion, they looked after their own people, and they had fine hospitals. At this she said that she wanted to be a hospital nurse, and the policeman smiled indulgently, and the sergeant said kindly that she had better stay in the merry-merry, which is an old slang-word for the chorus of a musical show, she would give us all such pleasure there. But the film star had frowned impatiently at the remark and presently said that we must be going.

Out in the car the foreigner was still asleep. As we started off again I said nervously, "I hope he is just asleep, I hope he's not ill." The film star said sleepily, "You're nervous, he's fine." The beautiful girl, with a curiously smooth and expert gesture, slid her fingers round the foreigner's wrist and took his pulse, and echoed, as sleepily, "He's fine." We left her at a little hotel near Grand Central Station and as she went in at the door she turned and gave us a sweet and empty smile. Then we turned down Park Avenue to drop the foreigner, and we wakened him. He came to himself with a start, just as we passed a huge illuminated clock-face. He uttered an exclamation and looked at his wrist-watch, raised his eyebrows, seemed to be calculating and then looked at his watch again. He gave a solemn shake of the head and I felt he was saying to himself, "It is no use at all trying to understand what happens on this side of the Atlantic, none at all."

I thought it probable that he understood French, but I did not feel equal to explaining just why such a long time had elapsed since we left the party. When he got out of the car he thanked us in a little speech, correctly pronounced and phrased, and I wondered again if after all he spoke English, but I think it was something he had learned by rote. He could not get into his hotel at once. Just before him someone had dashed in at such a pace that the revolving door was still spinning; and he stood and waited for it to slow down, his shoulders drooping with fatigue and impatience, the very image of a tired man far from home. He was thinking that where he came from revolving doors behaved more reasonably. The car turned towards my hotel, and the film star said, "It's been a grand evening. It was fun in the park. That's a sweet kid. But I wish she wouldn't plug that line about wanting to be a hospital nurse. It's corny."

But the beautiful girl was to surprise us all. I had misread the vacancy of her smile; it was empty only of guile, not of intelligence. She left the merry-merry and went into a Seventh Day Adventist hospital to train as a nurse; but somehow was deflected into laboratory work and became a physiologist. She worked in a research team that achieved some serious results and married a colleague and remained his assistant. But that was a revelation which was made only over the decades. The evening held a more immediate surprise for me. Two days later I met the host who had given the party and he said to me, "Isn't Pirandello a great guy?" I answered, "How should I know? I never met him." And Mike said, "Well, you took him home from my party."

[1] Charlie Chaplin, with whom Rebecca had had a romantic entanglement.

A DAY IN TOWN

From THE NEW YORKER, Jan. 25, 1941

Hour after hour throughout the night a German bomber cruised up and down over the moonlit beechwoods of our valley; and while it is easy enough to sleep through bombing in a shelter, it is difficult to get much sleep at all in a country house with hostile aircraft overhead, because an incendiary bomb would call for so much action. Therefore, I woke up to a crystal morning that had nothing of the uncertain dawn about it, and knew my plans for an early rising had gone wrong. And there was Winifred the housemaid beside my bed with my breakfast tray, saying with defiant dignity, "It is half past eight, Madam, I failed to hear the alarm clock."

She would have liked to be scolded; it would have made her feel that life was following its normal course. But knowing the cause of her sleeplessness, I was not equal to the gesture. So I said, "Well, then we obviously can't catch the 7:55 bus, and we obviously can't catch the 8:47 from High Dashwood. So tell the gardener's boy to cycle up to Mrs. Raven, and ask her if she can oblige us by driving us to the station in half an hour's time."

I poured the cream into my coffee and was reminded of my two cows: Primrose, an exquisite beige creature with immense eyelashes, slender ankles, a wittily held little head, and a general look of Ina Claire;

and Patience, a swarthy raw-boned being with a quick intelligent black eye and a bent muzzle, very like many an up and coming Jewish lawyer. The thought that they might be bombed or machine-gunned swept through me, and I was convulsed with sudden venomous hatred. I jumped out of bed, shuddering.

Winifred and I were dressed and ready to go when Mrs. Raven brought her Ford into the courtyard at the back of the house. But before we could leave we had to chase my ginger cat and lock him into the pantry, not to be released until my secretary came over from her cottage later. This crisis has revealed cats as the pitiful things they are: intellectuals who cannot understand the written or the spoken word. They suffer in these air-raids and the consequent migrations exactly as clever and sensitive people would suffer if they knew no history, had no conception of warfare, and could not be sure that those in whose houses they lived, on whose generosity they were dependent, were not responsible for their miseries. Had Pounce found himself alone in the house and free he would probably have lost faith in humans and their habitations and taken to the woods.

"Well, you've lost the 8:47," said Mrs. Raven with a chuckle. All over the world the most good-natured find enjoyment in those who lose trains or sit down suddenly on frozen pavements.

"Yes, we've lost the 8:47," I said, with the proper answering chuckle, and we loaded in the crate of vegetables I was taking up to my sister. We set off through the shining morning, with the sky an innocent blue over the thin gold plating of the stubble fields, the beechwoods warmed and rusting with autumn. It could have been pretended that England had not a trouble in the world, but for the nest of sandbags and barbed wire at the corners of the lanes. The Georgian red brick of High Dashwood was glowing rosily in the sunshine, the very colour of contentment. And luck was with us, for a London train was waiting for us in the station.

"What train is this?" I asked a porter, looking at my watch. It was twenty to ten.

"The 8:47," he said.

It was just as well I had not scolded Winifred. That's how it is in these days. The times make a fool of all one knew as order.

There were two men in our carriage. London office workers who had come out to stay with relatives in High Dashwood, because their homes were in the heavily bombed south areas of South London, and they had felt the need of unbroken sleep. "One night in five I must have," said the one, "so my old Auntie looks for me every five nights now." "I can't get more than one in six," said the other, "what with the home guard and all." They compared notes as to the easiest way of getting from point to point in the City, avoiding the damaged stations and the roped off areas. "Ah, but you haven't thought of Porkpie Passage. Never even heard of it, I don't suppose," the one said triumphantly, but broke off because, as the train was standing at a station, we heard the wail of the Air-raid warning. "They're late this morning," he said. From an aerodrome behind some houses a squadron of fighters was rising in battle formation, precisely aligned as ideal ballerinas.

Nothing worried these two very much, I gathered, except the delay in the mails, which they said showed faulty organization not to be explained by the present circumstances. They were still grumbling about it when we arrived at our terminus, which looked more cheerful than I have ever known it. This was because all the smoke-clouded glass in the vaults had gone, and the sunshine was pouring through the iron ribs. There were no taxis in the station, as it had been impossible to sweep up all the fine splinters of glass, so Winifred and I took each side of the crate and carried it outside. We dumped it at a corner and looked round for a taxi. The streets about seemed oddly empty. I assumed that there had been a bad raid last night, and that people were sleeping late.

Across a trafficless patch of street I saw a taxi, which had just deposited its fares at a house in a side street. I ran to pursue it, and while I was running the All Clear went. That is why I did not hear the shouts of the young policeman who presently caught me by the arm. "You're running straight towards a time-bomb. Can't you see that notice?" "No," I said, "I'm short-sighted." "Get some spectacles then," he said, and wiped his brow. "My God," he breathed, "you can move fast for your age."

We carried the vegetables for another block and found ourselves in a crowded street. Everyone wore the expression characteristic in a raided town. It is not unlike the look on the faces of pregnant women. It is as if they were drained of their strength by a condition against which there can be no rebellion, and of which they are not ashamed. We found a taxi that took us by unfamiliar ways to the square where we live. Down one of the streets that it avoided, though on the directest route, I saw a house where I have often dined, an empty shine between its neighbours, its familiar wallpapers brightly lining its nothingness.

About our apartments stood the janitors, pale and heavy eyed. The one that took our vegetables out of the taxi said, "A bomb fell in the square gardens last night, but only on the soft earth. Nobody was hurt and the glass hasn't gone." The old man who took us up in the elevator said, "Did you know that John Lewis has gone? It's gutted, gutted to the ground floor, and I nearly died of it. Just listen to what happened to me. You know me and my wife live at Harley Street. We're caretakers there now all the doctors are gone to the army. Well, what would my wife do except go every night to the shelter at John Lewis's. I often reasoned with her about it. 'What's the good of doing that?' I said. 'What's the good of going to a great place like that, which sticks up its head and asks to be bombed? Why not stay here, which is just a house among a thousand just the same? But she would have her way and went out every evening as soon as the Warning went. So last night I was sitting in our basement as snug as can be, and then I heard one of those awful bombs, and I said, 'Sure as knife's knife that's over by John Lewis's, and I run out into the street, and there I saw it blazing, and I ran along to the shelter, racing the way I haven't since I was a boy, and I said to the chap at the door of the shelter, I said, 'Look here, my wife's down there,' I said, and he said, 'Well, they're all coming out,' but believe me or not she was the very last one to come out, and when she came along I said to her, 'Well, where's your new rug and your new cushion that I bought you yesterday?' and she said, 'Oh, I was so upset I couldn't think of anything like that,' and of course, I couldn't be angry with her, being so glad she was all right, but this morning after breakfast, I said to her, 'Now you've got to go down to your sister at Chipping Norton as quick as we can put you on a train,' and I sent her off, for there's some people that can't cope with emergencies, and though she's been a good wife to me I don't feel she's been sensible, not over these raids."

Inside my apartment I looked at my shopping list with distaste and perplexity. I had meant to buy some more black-out lamp shades, some more china plates of a dinner-service, some electric light fittings, all from John Lewis; and I did not know where else I could get them. But I had not long to worry over that, for my butler was telling me that he could not go down to the country with us, because he might be called up at any minute. "But they haven't called up the thirty-nines yet, have they?" I asked. He answered that that was not the point. "The fact is, I am really a shipbuilder," he explained. He had gone into service only a few years before, in order to see life. "And have you seen more life being with us than you would have building ships?" I asked in bewilderment. "Oh, much," he said with conviction, but would not enlarge on the subject, for he had to tell me that he had registered some time before as one of those who could practice a craft of national importance, though they were not doing so now, and that in consequence he had been called up to undergo a medical examination the very next week.

I expressed my regret, which was real, but I had to hasten away to deliver the vegetables at my sister's apartment. She is a lawyer as well as a doctor, and she lives in one of those old Inns, as they were curiously called, which are inhabited chiefly by lawyers. She lives on the two top floors of the tall Regency house where Charles Dickens once worked as an office boy. I dragged the crate of vegetables up four flights, and the door was opened by the Austrian Jewish refugee who is her friend and does her housework, a coloured handkerchief about her head, a broom in her hand. She was a doctor of philology, she had been a happy and patient scholar in the field of medieval poetry. Now the opportunity to handle a broom represented an unhoped-for run of good luck. She murmured, "Ach, die gute Gemüse! We are so glad of them, for it is so hard to go out shopping now, whenever one takes one's basket and goes out the siren goes, and all the shops shut, and when the All Clear goes I am sure to be making jam, or seeing one of your sister's refugees."

But at that moment the Warning went, and I fled. All over London, when sirens go, people spring apart. If the warning finds one too far from home, one might be forced to take refuge in a public shelter, and waste precious hours; and when the All Clear sounds one runs out to take advantage of the opened shops and post-offices. My taxi whirled me homewards through poorer quarters than I had visited that day, where the damage had an unchivalrous air. At a corner, a rag and bone shop, and three storeys of frowsty lodgings over it, were still recognizable for what they were, but were twisted like barley sugar. It was not necessary to spoil what had in its essence never been unspoiled. During the latter part of the ride I made myself sick by swivelling round to look out of the back window, to see the trails of exhaust steam against the blue sky which marked a fight between a German and an English airman.

At home the butler gave me a luncheon of coffee, tinned tongue, and bread and jam, eaten off a tray in the lounge with machine-guns tapping at each other somewhere over the well of the apartment-house. I wondered how, with so much going on, I was to get up to Hampstead, where I was to have a conference with the friend who owns the paper of which I am an editor. But there was a telephone-ring, and it was my friend, who was not at Hampstead, but at her house in the country, for the excellent reason that there was a time-bomb in her Hampstead garden. We settled a matter of book reviews. Books, if they are books which treat of ideas, seem not less but rather more important than they did before; it is so obvious that this war is being fought between people who have different ideas about life. Then the All Clear sounded, and I ran out to seek substitute lampshades, to change books at the Times Book Club, to buy a chest of drawers I had seen in a shop-window and knew I needed for the new house.

While making that last purchase I realized that I was more shaken than I knew by the oddity of our times. The antique-dealer said to me, "No, I cannot let you have it for twelve pounds but I will give it you for thirteen," and I answered firmly though I knew I spoke like an idiot,

"No, I can't do that. I'll pay you twelve pounds nineteen shillings and eleven pence¹, but I won't pay you thirteen pounds."

Back in my apartment I found my husband sitting in the lounge. He had three days holiday before him, and was driving me back to the country. I thought he was looking rather pale, and I asked him if anything had happened. He said, "Yes. When I got to the Ministry this morning I found the whole front porch of the Ministry had been blown up. You have to go in at the back entrance. And I found that one of the men I liked best at the Ministry, an elderly man whom I really like and respected, had been killed."

The butler brought us in tea and said, "I was wondering if I might keep this as a souvenir, seeing that it fell in the kitchen." He held out to us a piece of shrapnel the size of a man's hand. "But did it not smash the window to smithereens?" I said. "It made a hole exactly like its own size," he replied, "but the splintered glass held. That varnish we painted the windows with has proved very serviceable."

While we were drinking our tea, my husband said, "Are those two women ready?" For we were taking down not only the housemaid, but the cook who, moved by affection for her married sister, whom she had not seen for as much as eight days, had been to spend the night with her in a suburb which for most of the twenty-four hours is the scene of appalling aerial warfare. "I can hear them packing up things in the kitchen," I said. "What things," he asked. "Extra china, cruets, boot polishing kit, all sorts of oddments we had forgotten in the new house," I said. "And we must take down some of your valuables," said my husband. "What would you like us to take?"

"Let us see," I said; and we pushed back the table and walked through the rooms. Everything we saw seemed victim of a sudden irreparable depreciation of value. It was no longer worth its price because of the people who lay under the whorled timber of the rag and bone shop. It was sometimes distressing because of other less corporeal deaths. We have a Rembrandt drawing, a tiny, cunning, living piece of magic, where a few strokes of a pencil show, receding into an immense distance, mile upon mile of Holland; we have a Dufuy that shows Burgundy as it is after the vines have had their copper sulphate spray, blue, deep bright blue, delphinium blue. They were portraits now of enslaved countries, unvisitable, dangerous.

Nothing in the apartment seemed to matter to me like the few fields we had in the country, like our Jersey cows or the bullocks we are fattening for autumn market, until we opened the drawing-room door and saw the long narrow Empire table which all through my married life has stood across the window. "Look at that!" I exclaimed. "What on earth has happened to it?" Its back was broken, each of the three panels which made up its top lay at an angle to the others. Its two wide legs were thrusting outwards, and the bar that joined them was ready to drop. I ran to it and found that every joint was gaping. Under the gentlest of blow, this beautifully and honestly made article of furniture would have fallen to pieces on the floor. I felt a sick yet distant anger that was extreme yet not quite my own, that might have been felt by the cabinet maker who made this table; and the butler said behind me: "It was like that when I came in this morning. I understand several people have noticed that the furniture nearest their windows has been affected like this. It has something to do with the blast." Beyond the window I could see London, obscured by the smoke that was still rising from the John Lewis store.

---

[1] In other words, one penny less than thirteen pounds. Until 1971, the UK used a "pounds, shillings and pence" system, where 12 pence made a shilling, and 20 shillings made a pound.

ASPECTS OF LOVE: MUTUAL DISLIKE

PARADISE LOST, by John Milton,
PUNCH, Feb. 6, 1963

I frequently read *Paradise Lost*, sometimes for the noble phrase and splendid line and the bellyflop (but such a magnificent belly) into bathos, and sometimes as a gloss on the day's newspapers. There is nothing like it for illumining the mysteries of war. Milton knew it all. Anybody who has read *Paradise Lost* (and turned to the confirming testimony provided by a different temperament in *Troilus and Cressida*) knows all about what happened between 1914 and 1918, between 1939 and 1945, and since then on to Katanga. From Milton's report of the organ-toned argy-bargying of super-terrestrial egos anybody could have foretold the style and contents of the generals' memoirs, the disputes between the different branches of the Armed Forces, the intrigues of the Pentagon, and what has been happening lately in the United Nations. Field-Marshal Montgomery is primarily someone whom Shakespeare and Milton omitted for lack of space, but Milton did deal with Dr. Conor O'Brien[1], though he failed to mention his nationality.

But he is also very good on one aspect of love, though extremely alarming. I often go back to the parts of *Paradise Lost* which deal with love, just to see that I have not made a mistake, and to wonder why it is allowed to be read in girls' schools, and whether there is any escape from the disagreeable conclusions with which it fills my mind.

Milton could not take a wide survey of love, because he was allergic to amiability, but one aspect he covered thoroughly, and that an aspect others have been too self-conscious to discuss with candour. This achievement is hard to discover, because the characters are disguised. He calls them Adam and Eve although they have little to do with Adam and Eve of the Bible. That is apparent as the iambic pentameters creak under the couple's heavy tread, for it cannot be denied that the Biblical Adam and Eve were young. The terrible thing about their story, our story, is that they were juvenile delinquents. But Adam is plainly Milton and many men who, like Milton when he wrote *Paradise Lost*, are over fifty, and Eve is all the women who had been in his life, or ever would be, or nearly were—the three Mrs. Miltons and the candidates who failed or did not choose to sit their finals, and the poor women are as he saw them when he was over fifty and apt, as the less amiable sorts of men are as time passes, to lend women some of their age when they look at them.

Milton's Adam and Eve are not young; they have been together a long time. And they do not like each other any more. They never liked each other very much, and long companionship, and the disagreeable elements in both their characters, have matured their dislike into a formidable and vigilant hostility, of the god-fearing sort that makes its demonstrations oblique. When Adam and Eve speak to one another they always begin by a statement of devotion which can only mean that this emotion has left them for ever. When does one describe one's dog clearly and in detail? Only when inserting an advertisement under the "Lost Dog" heading in the local newspaper. "Sole partner and sole part of all those joys, Dearer thyself than all..." "Thou for whom and from whom I was form'd flesh of thy flesh And without whom am to no end, my Guide and Head..." "My Author and Disposer, what thou bidst Unargu'd I obey..." There is nothing unnatural in these sentiments, cherished at one time or another by all except the unluckiest among us, but when they are genuine they come up in the conversation according to the delightful logic of the moment. They are not nervously recited at the beginning of each speech as if in fear of what might be said before it ended. "O Thou in whom my thoughts find all repose, My Glory, My Perfection," was spoken by Eve not in circumstances admitting the possibility of ecstasy, but when she had just been awakened by Adam with a suggestion that they get on with some early morning gardening.

The full horror of this union is crystallised (as is often the case in life) when a visitor is introduced into their home. Those of us who have been on lecturing tours have sometimes found as we shyly entered the houses of our unknown hosts that we have been the last straw, and that is why experienced speakers elect to stay in hotels, where there are no camels' backs. The Almighty sent down the angel Raphael to explain the Universe to Adam; and Adam sees and identifies the super-terrestrial splendour coasting down through the trees. It is not as irrelevant as it might seem to note that Milton was learned in cabalistic literature; for it has been suggested of late that the tradition of angelic visits found in ancient cultures springs from recollections of visits from space travellers sent by some highly developed planets long ago. Unnecessarily, as Eve was competent though dull, Adam ordered Eve to get a good meal ready, "to go with speed and what thy stores contain bring forth and pour Abundance." Eve snapped back that she has no stores. They are unnecessary since everything "Ripe for use hangs on the stalk. Save," she added with insufferable domestic-economy-teacher knowingness, "what by frugal storing firmness gains / To nourish, and superfluous moist consumes." The lines crackle with hatred.

The meal was evidently satisfactory, except for Adam's conversation. He asked the angel indiscreet questions about the meals served in heaven, without being able to disguise his desire to know (and of course he had a good point here) how incorporeal beings managed to digest their food. The angel answered vaguely and decisively, like a well-bred person parrying tactless curiosity, and went on to fulfill his very difficult mission. He had to warn Adam that though he had been given free will by the Almighty, this would not exempt him from punishment if he chose to will the wrong thing, and he had to emphasise how serious these matters are by recounting the history of Lucifer's rebellion, and then put things in as good a light as possible by describing the glories of Creation.

He made a magnificent job of it; and Adam took this revelation of the kind of universe he had been let in for with what may have been courage or insensibility. He then asked the angel some questions about astronomy which received a reply aimed straight through time at the heart of Dr. Bronowski.[2] As Milton put it in his prose gloss on the poem, Adam was "exhorted to search rather things more worthy of knowledge," and he accepted the advice by consulting the angel on his sexual life, at enormous length, for it was much on his mind; so much that Eve may well have been not only the first woman but the first woman to express the opinion that Men Want Only One Thing.

She may also have been the first woman to use the phrase "I've Never Been so Insulted in my Life." For in this conversation Adam cut away the moral supports that prop up the life of man and woman. He explained that he asked the Almighty to provide him with a mate only because he found the society of the tame animals with which Paradise was stocked insufficiently entertaining. Eve was not there to hear this, assuring Adam that she would far rather hear the conversation from him afterwards than listen to it herself. Of course this chatter-box took her at her word and repeated it, and she cannot have been pleased to hear that Adam had had her created because Zoos are not enough. He was also most unpleasant about his sexual relations with Eve, taking it hard that he sometimes found himself not so pompous as usual when he was in bed with her. "All higher knowledge in her presence falls Degraded, Wisdom discount'nanc't, and like folly shews." What should he do about it? The angel said not to worry. The thing is, if Adam found himself taking sex too seriously, to reflect that it cannot matter much, since it has been vouchsafed also to Cattle and each Beast.

This was the best answer to give Adam. But the angel was swiftly punished, for Adam's indiscretion took charge of him again and he asked the angel whether this sort of thing occurred in heaven. The angel turned pink ("with a smile that glow'd Celestial rosy red, Love's proper hue") and replied that that was all right, thank you. He then made some curious remarks about certain refinements which he claimed were practised by Celestial beings, remarked "But I can now no more," and pointed out that the sun was setting, and he must go on the return journey. He probably was a space-traveller, and rather a young one.

We know quite well that Adam would call Eve out of the garden and go over the conversation, and that she would not appreciate it. "Well, Eve, that was an intelligent young man. It does one good to have a talk sometimes with someone who lives such a different life and has been to all those places, and really understands politics. And I think he enjoyed himself." "Do you? I'm not so sure about that." "What can you mean?" "Well, you shouldn't have talked to him as you did. I didn't know where to look when you asked him all those things about his digestion, whether he didn't drink milk because it was constipating, and if he found radishes repeated. And now you tell me you asked him all these things about whether the native women out there were attractive. He'd see what you were driving at, and I don't believe he'd like it." "Nonsense, nonsense. He's broad-minded enough to stand that. He's a man of the world. And anyway I didn't mean it like that." However, she would not like the set piece that was designed to justify the ways of God to man. "Well, if that's what the lease really means all I can say is that it's a very tricky one, and all those rows and fighting, this isn't nearly such a nice neighbourhood as we thought. I told you we ought to be more careful." They would bicker on like people in a Sickert drawing[3], and then silence would fall, and Adam would say to himself, "She never understands, she spoils everything," while she was thinking the same thing about him. Their dislike was dislike, looked at from any angle.

Yet the next day, when Eve wanted to garden in a different part of Paradise ("I was thinking, why don't we try taking our holidays separately this year?"), Adam was hurt. Milton is with him and represents her as moved by a desire to get away and conspire with the serpent.

And what was the serpent? Why, nothing to do with the knowledge of good and evil. That Adam already had, he could not have known how to be a prig without it. The serpent in all Paradises is not a condition of the mind but a matter of hard fact: the power possessed by any human being to leave another human being who does not want to be left. When Adam became aware of Eve's desire for separateness, when weak females flagged and failed under the intolerable burden of being one with Milton, Adam and Milton suffered as if they felt the serpent's fang. Yet Adam did not like Eve and Milton could not like any woman. (Sonnets addressed to wives who are dead at the time of writing are not evidence.)

Here we come on the overwhelming paradox of *Paradise Lost*. Milton made Adam do more for Eve than any hero of legend or literature had done for any woman since Orpheus; and he comes in far ahead of Orpheus, for he carried off his great feat and Orpheus muffed his. Milton's Adam ate the forbidden fruit, although he knew it was a sin and had no disposition to commit that sin; conceit was his grand transgression. He ate the forbidden fruit knowing the punishment, simply because he wished to suffer the same penalty as guilty Eve, and be driven with her out of Paradise. He did not wish to lose her and he could not bear to think of her wandering alone in the wilderness. This sacrifice is unique. There is no male equivalent of Alcestis or Antigone; the gentlemen in Shakespeare's plays do nothing for ladies but cause them the maximum of picturesque inconvenience; it is a marvel how Racine's gentlemen and the society they compose treat their ladies so rough while keeping their alexandrines so smooth. It would seem clear that men do not love women enough to pay ransom for them in the real hard currency of sacrifice, and Adam and Milton were glorious exceptions. But they were horrible exceptions too. The works of the classical dramatists and Shakespeare and Racine could be searched in vain for men supposed to be good, not admitted to be very bad indeed, who treated their wives with the steady, devouring dislike which Adam showed for Eve.

The situation, like so many arising out of the relationship between men and women, is so contradictory that no conclusion can be drawn from it. Do men love women? Do women love men? Do they like each other? If they do not, then why do they persist through the centuries in not only mating but marrying? And how does it happen that there are such wide differences between the minds and character of the sexes that marriage is difficult? How is it that the two halves of a species can have desires so incompatible and be so limited in their capacity to understand each other?

I myself have been haunted by a theory which accounts for it, ever since I read, in *Planète*, a highly entertaining French journal of popular science, an article on the work of Dr. Agrest, an Armenian physicist, who works in the Soviet Union. It is entirely the fault of my lightmindedness that I imagine him as looking like the Sorcerer who owned the puppets in *Petrushka*. He is certainly a quite serious scientist. It appears there are scattered over the world vitreous areas containing radio-active elements, not volcanic in origin, which Dr. Agrest believes to be due to the operations of space-ships sent out by an advanced planet which landed on this earth long ago, in the early days of human civilisation. He believes that the space-travellers imparted information about the physical universe to human beings which these then lacked, and were even unable to confirm till centuries had passed; this would explain how some astronomical bodies invisible to the naked eye were known to the ancients.

This idea has been seized on by some to explain the persistent tradition of angelic visits, and it certainly suggests that there may have been a specific legend behind Milton's account of Raphael's visit to Adam, even to the oddest details. It must have been disconcerting for a pedagogic space-traveller, as it might be for Dr. Bronowski, to try to impart scientific information to a nude, verbose, and self-satisfied patriarch, really only interested in his own sex life, and surrounded by wild animals behaving oddly (th' Unwieldy Elephant to make them mirth us'd all his Might & Wreath'd His Lithe Proboscis). Small wonder if the space-traveller gave up and advised Adam to think no more about it.

But I think they went further than that. Obviously they would think little of us; and they would on the facts have classified this as a backward planet. We all know what that leads to. We would be meat for some interplanetary organization that sought to develop us, and this one tampered with earth's population. Probably we were multiplying more quickly or more slowly than they thought was wise, and heaven knows there are plenty of defects they might have noticed. Anyway, I think they decided we might breed better if we were hybridised with the inhabitants of some other planet, and our blood X was mixed with blood Y, alien by some million light-years. It did not work too badly, but it did not work too well. We go into marriage in the hope of the simple union which was doubtless the rule when we were all X's marrying X's, but which is now a rare hope, since each of us is X plus Y, mixed in an unknown proportion, entailing an unforeseeable, unpreventable amount of incomprehension. Doubtless this could all be set right if the space-travellers would come back; in that advanced planet, science must really by this time have advanced so far as to be able to correct its mistakes. There, anti-fallout makes the popular beautiful and healthy, myxomatosis[4] makes real rabbits as amenable as toys, and so on, including this purging of confusion from our blood. But Dr. Agrest explains that space-travellers probably have not even got home yet to report, owing to a hitch in interplanetary time. This last detail convinces me of the truth of his theories and of mine. This is the universe we know, the universe which Milton attempted to justify: most interesting, but with no consideration at all.

O'Brien led the United Nations operation in the Congo in 1960, was Ireland's minister … photographs in the mid-1970s and became editor-in-chief of The Observer newspaper in 1979 for three years. He … d Dec. 19, 2008.

… British Mathematician, Biologist, and Blake scholar, the driving … behind the BBC television series … he Ascent of Man."

… 1921 was a German-born English Impressionist painter. … m and … who favoured ordinary people and urban … proportions.

WHY MY MOTHER WAS FRIGHTENED OF CATS

[From typewritten manuscript, 1956]

For me to keep a cat has all the excitement of a forbidden love-affair, for my mother belonged to that unhappy race which feels a mysterious fear of cats. If she found herself in a room with the most innocent and ravishing of cats, she would start to her feet and wring her hands, the long supple hands of a pianist, and she would cry, "Take it away! Take it away!" while she shut her eyes so that she need not see the loathsome object. I never reproached my mother even in my own mind for these paroxysms, for I was a soldier's daughter, and it was well-known that the most venerable general of that day, Lord Roberts, suffered from the same malady. He would turn and run if a cat walked towards him on the parade-ground; and I quite realised that if Lord Roberts could not control this terror my mother could not be expected to do better. So there was no ill-feeling between us.

Yet not to have a cat inflicted a great hardship on me. Ever since I was a little child I have thought cats the most beautiful and alluring of created beings. It has been in some ways a protection to me. I have never felt jealous of other women because they were more beautiful

32

than I was, for almost any cat was far more beautiful than either me or them. Nor have I ever felt that disillusionment which other wives feel at unromantic moments of domestic life, when, for example, their husbands walk about in short dressing-gowns which show the striped legs of pyjamas. I know I must accept the second-rate in these matters, since I could never be the mate of a beautiful tom-cat who has for permanent wear a shining garment of silky fur moulding to a symphony of sliding muscles. But my belief has left me with an abiding sorrow because I was not born a cat, and I felt very badly used because I could not do the next best thing and keep a cat until my mother died; and that various inconvenient circumstances prevented me from acquiring one till long after that date. Then I felt it was too late. I was like a woman who had wanted children all her life and at last finds herself free to become a mother and then feels panic. I thought I would never be able to rear a cat, I felt sure I would give it the wrong food, I saw a stern vet reproaching me by my cat's basket and asking me if I had not let my professional duties come between my duty to my cat.

But my son had a cat, and when he went on a holiday he called on me and dropped the cat into the drawing-room window, saying, "Look after Poughkeepsie till I come back." Poughkeepsie is the name of an American town, a delightful name in English wars, for it is an Indian name and evokes the charm of Fenimore Cooper and the United States when they were innocent and idyllic. But far from looking like anything in rural nineteenth century America, Poughkeepsie was the double of Martine Carol[1]. I did not recognise the resemblance, for this happened some time ago, when Martine Carol was in her cradle or thereabouts. But Poughkeepsie had the same perpetual air of being at once surprised and never at a loss; and she had the same trim compactness of body, which put into everybody's head the idea that it would be charming to pick her up and carry her about.

She enchanted us, and settled all my misgivings. I never had to worry about her diet. It was the season of grouse. She consented to eat grouse and she even helped me by indicating that she preferred grouse to any other form of food. She also indicated that she preferred to eat in the drawing-room. So it happened that some strangers who

33

visited us said afterwards, "They seem quite nice people but why do they keep a dish of cold grouse on the piano?" As to letting my professional duties come before my duty to my cat, my cat let her social duties come before her duty to me. She had put a paw in the field of human interests in a way that seemed very odd to me then. From time to time she strayed and paid visits on our neighbours, and exercised a very curious discrimination concerning the neighbours whom she honoured. Our clergyman was fond of cats, the village school-mistress adored them and was in an emotional state about them, having just lost her old tabby, and our washerwoman, who told fortunes, treated animals as witches treat their familiars. But none of these was visited by Poughkeepsie. First she sought out the doctor. I am forced to mention that he had married money and had a beautiful Queen Anne house. She also visited the lord of the manor, who kept two manservants, while we had only one. Then she went a mile up the road, though she was afraid of the traffic, and introduced herself to the Duchess. So obviously was Poughkeepsie trying to improve her social position that there could be no doubt that somehow or other she had grasped what a social position was.

My son retrieved her on his return from his holiday. On seeing him, Poughkeepsie sat down and washed her face. She was plainly in no hurry to leave a household where there was cold grouse on the piano and ample opportunities for introducing oneself to the *gratin*. But my son was a virile young man, six foot tall, and attractive in the style of Mr. Rochester; and Poughkeepsie suddenly took a flying leap on to his knee. Probably in every species each sex thinks its opposite not quite what it would have ordered, and thinks that other species do better. She left us without a backward glance, and I have an impression that I carried her expensive luggage out to the automobile with her, and that she did not thank me.

This was, of course, not a serious relationship, not a true sample of the joys and sorrows which cats can bring us. It was the equivalent of the love-affair with a chorus-girl which is not so much love as an introduction to the technique of love. But I did not understand that, and when my son offered me one of Poughkeepsie's kittens I accepted it in the belief that it would give the same sort of pleasure as its mother. But the first sight of the kitten dispelled this idea. He was physically frivolous, a ball of orange fluff with topaz eyes, he might have been the sort of Christmas present the more expensive stores in New York think up, and have a bottle of scent inside him; yet he was a serious-minded cat. When he looked at one, he referred what he saw to a store of innate knowledge and a firm tradition, and passed a judgment on one which he at once prudently put by for later use. There was also a sense of frustration about him which seemed to spring from his inability to take part in the conversation. Without doubt, cats are intellectuals who have been, by some mysterious decree of Providence, deprived of the comfort of the word.

He at once, by a single action, declared his character and moulded it. We had bought a new house, but could not get into it, and in the meantime had taken a house of a more seigniorial sort than we ordinarily inhabited. Our gardens were superb. Poughkeepsie had had social ambitions but not a rag of pedigree; and the father of this new kitten had been a farm labourer, who earned a meager living by keeping down the rats in a granary. The kitten's name was plain Pounce, as it might have been Untel[2]. But the grandeur of the surroundings was entirely to his taste. He did not merely accept them, he savoured them, he turned them over on his tongue. Out he went across the lawn with the two cedars, down the stone steps to the terrace with its high banks of lupins, his tail straight up and swaying with satisfaction. Along the yew walk he went to the rose-garden, not hurrying it, taking it at a processional pace, past the carrousel of lily-beds to the lake of nenuphars. There he went too far. The tiny creature leaped to the furthest conceivable extreme of ambition. He tried to walk on the water.

Before we could get to him he was a snuffling and scrambling rag of wet fur. Somebody had laughed. His pride was cut to the quick. "You needn't help me! I can get out by myself! Let go!" He started back to the house, careful not to hurry and lose his dignity, and keeping his tail upright and waving, though it was a miserable little stump. How should a kitten grasp the idea of "making a fool of oneself," with all its implications, which involve self-respect, the importance we attach to the opinion of others, and our tendency to laugh when someone has a physical misadventure? But all this Pounce realised, and more besides. He had tried to walk on something that looked as solid as a floor, and it had not borne his weight as it had promised but had let him fall through into a horrible engulfing element that had made him cold and wet and ridiculous, and people had burst out laughing, and there had been nothing to do but walk on and pretend that nothing had happened. For ever after Pounce was a stoic and a cynic. In later years he used to kiss my hand when I stroked him. But always before the kiss he gave me a hard stare. "If I give her an inch, will she take an ell? Will she trespass on the secret places of my being if I let her be too familiar?" He took the risk, but he was always sensible that it was a risk.

This reserve and withdrawal were the more fascinating because he was a superb comedian, specialising in a sort of gymnastic satire. The house where we were living was not as good as its gardens, for its owner had allowed an interior decorator to transform its seventeenth-century rooms into the stage set of a provincial production of *Cyrano de Bergerac* or *The Three Musketeers*. The place was cluttered with refectory tables and high-backed chairs which evoked bad actors sweeping off huge hats adorned with moulting feathers and declaiming alexandrines at bad actresses sweeping blowsy curtseys. These were depressing surroundings, particularly when the summer ended and war broke out, and we were unable to move away. But they were lightened by the athletic ridicule with which Pounce treated this furniture which was worse than Porte St. Martin stuff, because it was obviously very expensive. He was at his best with an atrocity peculiar to England, the apotheosis of the bogus picturesque, called the Knole settee. It is the copy of a kind of sofa which was made in the seventeenth century, before cabinet-makers had learned how to make sofas, and it is neither beautiful nor comfortable, for its sides and back are not joined by carpentry but are held together with thick silken ropes. It owes its preservation only to the snobbery of the antique. All this Pounce seemed to say, as he swung from the silken ropes, balanced on them, sprang from them to the next article of furniture to be mocked.

It was all the more amusing because his pranks had the quality of wit that is too subtle to wound. He weighed nothing and his paws were too young and soft to leave scratches. The owner of the house never knew what Pounce had thought of her treasures.

It is easy to say that Pounce had formed no critical judgment of the furniture, and that we ascribed wit to him only because he was lithe and quick as we imagine wit would be if it had a corporeal shape. It was not easy to maintain that scepticism if one lived with Pounce. At least one had to admit that a comic genius was presiding over Pounce's destiny. There was, for example, the mistake made by the vet.

Nocturnal scufflings in the night, and a horrid rent in one of Pounce's exquisitely shaped ears, made me realise that I must have him doctored. I would gladly have left him the pleasures of love, but on the other hand it was cruel to ask Voltaire to live the life of Casanova. He went to the vet and stayed with him for two days. When he returned we noted two things: a new lustre on his fur which we had not remarked before, and a strange contentment, not quite of the sort we would have expected as the result of his new state. This was not resignation. Rather did it remind me of the active gloating which I had noted in a famous lawyer when I sat with him in his garden the day after he had vanquished his only serious rival at the bar. We had another surprise during the night, when there were again scufflings in the shrubbery, again love cries. But one of the gardeners had a tom-cat. All the same, Pounce was out and did not come back till morning.

Then a note came from the vet. There had been a mistake that for him was terrible. At the same time that we had left Pounce at the surgery, the vet had received a superb young tom-cat, the offspring of a champion sire and dam, himself destined to be a champion sire, in order that he should be put in perfect condition for his first show. By some extraordinary accident the pedigree tom had been castrated and the plebeian Pounce had been groomed for appearance at a show which would never have let him inside its doors.

Obviously this accident was the result of carelessness on the part of the vet's assistants. Pounce cannot really have said to the pedigree tom: "Look here, old man, I can let you in on a good thing. They're going to do an operation on me which doesn't hurt, and it means I'll be on velvet for the rest of my life. Now, I like you, I can see you're a thoroughly good chap, and I'll let you have the operation instead of me, if you like. It will mean I will have to wait my turn, but I don't care, I'm the sort of man who enjoys doing a friend a favour." Yet, as we took him to the vet for the second time, there was a gloomy composure and defiant humour in his limpid stare. He might have been saying, "Well, I couldn't expect to get away with it forever. But at any rate, you weren't able to do me out of that last night in the shrubbery."

Never did Pounce simply live. He always made a comment on life as he lived it. He was destined to be heroic as well as comic, for soon after this we went back to our apartment in London, and the battle of Britain burst on us, without succeeding in ruffling Pounce's whiskers. But he was not merely imperturbable. When the night was made hideous with big guns and high-explosive bombs, he would pace the rocking floor with cynical panache, as if he were saying, "You humans are an odd species, always up to something, and all this does me much less harm than the fuss you kick up when I help myself to a bit of chicken off the kitchen table." Ignoring the war, and deprived of the promenades and the sporting pursuits he had enjoyed in the country, he abandoned himself to the only line now left to him, and he looked for a human being to adore. He chose my husband. He lay at my husband's feet during breakfast, and would go with him to the front door when it was time for him to go to his work. Then came the comment. The door once closed, he would slowly turn round and cross the hall to the sofa, and curl up on its cushions with a sad little shake of the head. "There is nothing to do but sleep till he comes back."

I was wounded a little when he decided not to make me the object of his adoration. I was content to love rather than be loved, and he was really very kind and companionable. I had much to contend with at this time, for I was ill and should have had an operation, but put it off because I wanted to finish a book on which I had already spent some years. I used to sit nearly all day in a big armchair, writing in a folio exercise book, my books of reference on the floor around me, and often I broke off because I felt afraid that we would lose the war or that I would die and leave my book unfinished. At such times it was a great comfort to have Pounce asleep in the armchair beside me, relaxed as surely no such intelligent animal would be unless it had an assurance that all things would end well. He was really very kind to me. I used to wonder why my mother, who was right about almost everything, should have been so wrong about cats.

Then suddenly a disquieting fact was brought to my notice. We lived on the top floor of the apartment house, and outside our windows a cornice ran round the four sides of the building. This Pounce used as a playground, to take the air and exercise his sense of power by ordering the pigeons he found there to take off into the empyrean, and we used to watch him complacently. But it now appeared that he had been using the cornice for other and odious purposes. He had been visiting a neighbour of ours. Not all our neighbours, only one. He had walked past the window of hosts who would have been glad to entertain him, who cried "Pussy, pussy" as he went by, imagining him to be innocent and playful like themselves, and he went round two sides of the building to the apartment furthest from ours, to call on Mr. Gubbins: the one person among our neighbours who belonged to the same unhappy race as my mother, who feared cats.

The abominable genius of Pounce not only led him to this victim but indicated to him the moments when he was alone and most vulnerable. The poor man suffered from the fear of cats in an even more intense form than my mother. When he saw a cat he became paralysed. Pounce used to visit him when he was having a bath. Mr. Gubbins was not favoured by nature. He was an industrialist who looked like a Communist cartoonist's victim of a wicked capitalist: a tall and flabby man, with pouches under his pale eyes and drooping cheeks and chins and paunch, and the unpleasant peculiarity that his wispy moustache and strands of hair combed across his bald scalp were bright gold like the yolk of an egg. When Pounce dropped into his bathroom and sat down on his haunches and looked at Mr. Gubbins, the poor man's deplorable and pendulous nakedness was then congealed. The poor man could not get to his bath-towel, to his bell, to his door; he could only utter loud wordless groans for help. If his door was locked, he had to stay where he was until his manservant crawled out on the cornice and released him. And Pounce had always left before the manservant arrived.

The poor man learned to keep his windows shut. But Pounce learned that he could still reduce Mr. Gubbins to immobility by crouching on the cornice and staring in through the glass. Once his victim nearly fainted in his bath owing to this silent and murderous survey. He took to drawing his curtains, but Pounce serenaded him and by now had complete emotional control of the situation, and the mere sound of his meowing made Mr. Gubbins very ill. At this point the inhumanity of our own species took a hand. Mr. Gubbins could not discover where Pounce came from. He questioned the porters, but they denied all knowledge of any marmalade cat in the building. Unimaginative men, they thought it foolish of Mr. Gubbins to make a fuss about a cat in the middle of an air-war, and they attributed his fear of his visitor, very unkindly, to the fumes of brandy that were apt to hang about poor Mr. Gubbins when came down to the shelter at night. He would have never known how to find his tormentor if he had not seen a photograph of me and my cat outside a photographer's office.

When I received the letter from Mr. Gubbins which told me of this shocking sadistic crime, the criminal was sitting at my feet. Never had he looked more beautiful. The subtle lines of his muscle gave him a strong resemblance to Sarah Bernhardt in her youth; his fur, orange and gold and flame and snow-white, had the brilliance and lustre and depth which is given by health and youth; and his purr had the tone of a cello. I gasped. Lovely, and so odious! Then, accepting for a moment the conventional view of an animal's limitations, I wondered how I could bring his crime home to him. I could not, after all, take him along to Mr. Gubbins' apartment and, entering the bathroom, point to Mr. Gubbins' nakedness and indicate that this was something tabu, like the china and glass objects in our drawing room and the food on the kitchen table. But I need not have troubled. As soon as I recited the story to my husband, Pounce knew what I was talking about. He raised his exquisite muzzle and fixed me with his limpid stare and licked his whiskers with his pink tongue. "But it was such fun," he was saying.

"If you could have seen him! And what does it matter if a person like that suffers? Ignoble individual, unworthy personage that he is, what good is he, except to amuse me?"

I knew then that my mother had had some cause for her fear of cats.

Mercifully, I was soon able to remove Pounce out of the way of temptation, for our own house in the country became available. Once we were installed there he again became innocent. In spring he knew an ecstasy that made me think of Ronsard or the medieval Latin poets when they wrote of roses. He loved autumn too, and loved to lie among the red beech-leaves that were the same colour as himself. In winter the warm radiators tempted him to be lazy, they made such good beds, but even then the garden offered him delirious joys. On a moonlit night, when the snow lay thick, the shadow of a great pine lay in a blue bar across the lawn. Along this corridor Pounce crept as if there and there only lay safety from cunning enemies, then dashed out into the woods beyond and found a clearing where he performed the wild ritual dance they had sought to prevent him from achieving. He was a great dramatist, a great actor. When the fern grew high on the asparagus bed he could be seen in the middle of its shade, his narrow eyes burning with hope and despair.

Quite without warning, he lost his great passion for my husband; it was as if he had coldly said to himself that it could lead to nothing. But he was always kind to us. Even when the garden and the woods were most alluring he made a point of coming into the drawing-room at tea-time and having a saucer of milk, very much as Victorian parents always made a point of having their children brought down from the nursery for an hour between five and six. The family had to be kept together. He was always very kind to us when we were ill, and would come and lie on our beds, though he would do that at no other time. But always in his expressions remained a measure of reserve. He never lost his fear that if he encouraged us we might get too familiar. When we had been in London and he heard the horn of our automobile, he always recognised it and would rush out into the yard. But as we got out of the automobile he would turn his back on us and walk slowly away, as if he had been there by pure chance. One could not be too careful.

He was a great and classic hunter. When he killed a bird or a rabbit he would parade in front of the house with it in his mouth and then lay it down on the stone terrace under the room where I work, and put back his head and chant, "Look! Look! This is Pounce, the magnificent Pounce, lord of the fields and the woods, and this is his kill! Look, and give praise to him who deserves it!" And he would go on till I had put my head out of the window. But I never enjoyed his hunting. For one thing, he brought the rabbits into the house, and preferred to eat them on our best carpets. We would chase him off the Savonnerie and find he had gone round to the other side of the house and was eating it on the Empire Aubusson. It was unfortunate too that a whole rabbit was too much for him. He never could manage the last leg, and he had found a perfect place for storing this joint, between a Chippendale bookcase and the wall. He was always furious when he found that this tid-bit had been removed. "What is the use of my trying to bring some sense of order into this house, which is so frightfully untidy with all these books and papers, if people interfere with all my arrangements?" His hunting was natural, the most natural thing in the world; but it was inconvenient, and sometimes it made me remember Mr. Gubbins.

But one summer morning I woke up very early, and as the weather had been hot I resolved to go down into the garden and do some weeding among the raspberry canes while it was still cool. It was perhaps five o'clock. As I went through the orchard, the grass was wet and the birds were singing with the boisterousness which means that man is not yet about. I had been working for some time among the tall raspberry canes when I saw Pounce coming out of the woods and up the grassy slope towards the fruit-garden. He was walking tiger-wise, low to the ground, his head thrust out and his ear pricked and his whiskers bristling. In front him he was driving a young rabbit. Keepers tell they have often seen this, but that does not lessen the mystery of what I saw. The young rabbit, shivering, was walking a foot or so ahead of the cat as if he had been told to go toward the house and keep going. It was making no effort to escape. This was an event in the same category as the arrest of a young and idealistic and terrified political prisoner.

I kept quite still behind the raspberry canes and waited for the right moment to intervene. But as they got near me, Pounce halted and lay down, and so, after a moment, did the rabbit. The sun was coming up yellow over the hills and Pounce turned his head towards the sunshine. The rabbit continued to tremble, its terror shook it with a strength that one would not have thought its weakness could engender. Pounce lay there for some moments, and then got up and went towards the rabbit, which became rigid. I was about to shout, when he walked past the rabbit without touching it. Slowly the rabbit cast off its paralysis, it struggled to its legs, its muzzle twitching. For a time it wobbled, and then, desperately, as if it were fleeing for life instead of turning its back on it, it lollopped after Pounce. But after a yard or two Pounce wheeled round on it and spat. I held my head between my hands. This was all as bizarre as if they had started talking to each other. The rabbit fell shuddering back on its haunches, and Pounce strode on into the orchard. But again the rabbit got on its legs and pursued its captor. It could be seen how badly made a rabbit is, compared to a cat; it has really no card to play except its pathos. This time Pounce was really angry. He waited till the rabbit came quite near and then his paw flashed out and caught it on the muzzle. The rabbit rolled over and lay panting and emitting a thin, high sound, while Pounce slowly went through the orchard back to the house, treading down the long morning shadows cast by the apple-trees.

I had stumbled upon some stage of a process which I cannot understand. Pounce had looked as if he were saying, "You little fool, don't you see I can't be bothered with you? Go away. I don't want to kill you." But why should a cat feel this cruel kind of mercy for a rabbit? I was standing on the edge of a territory about which I knew nothing, about which I could guess nothing. Yet theoretically all Pounce's intellectual processes were simpler than mine, and I had known him for years.

At last there came a time when we noted that Pounce's fur was not so brilliant as it had been, that his profile was blunted and no longer recalled the young Sarah Bernhardt, that when he wanted to come in from the garden he mewed for us to open the French window, instead of jumping up to the little high window we always left wide for him. A visitor said, "That cat is beginning to look his age," and our hearts contracted. But he had a very happy old age. He was the very pattern of a crusty but contented old bachelor. He took great care of himself; when the wind rattled the shutters on the front of the house he would ask us to let him out by the back door. He was particular about his food; and if he disliked the meal the servants put out for him he could come to me with the expression of an outraged gourmet. He liked the house to be quiet, and was uncivil to the guests when we had parties. He loathed any manifestation of the publicity which was the result of my profession, and spat and sulked when he saw cameras being installed. When I forced him to pose for a specially gifted photographer who wanted to portray him in colour, I had to struggle with him till my dress was twisted round me in corkscrew folds. He gave me to understand that this was not the sort of thing that should happen to a cat of standing in his own house.

But his heart mellowed. He formed a deep though not effusive friendship with our black Labrador. "He may be a dog," he said, "but at least he is a gentleman." He even fell in love again with a human being. A Frenchwoman married to a Scotsman, Madame McVey came to be my cook, a charming creature who moved quickly like a cat and painted delicate watercolours that might have been the work of a cat's paw. He felt an old man's deep and wistful passion for her, but he was still kind to me. I sleep badly, and often I work late; and often when I left my study to go up to bed I would find him waiting outside my door, and he would get up and stretch and rub against my legs, and say, "Since you are late, you might as well be a little later, and get me something to eat." Then we went into the kitchen and he would lie down by the warm stove while I went into the pantry and cut him a slice off the rationed joint or opened a tin of rationed sardines or whatever else I could find that was too good for a cat. He always ate this morsel with a certain zestful deliberation. Both of us were enjoying our complicity in this small crime while everyone else in the house was sleeping. Then I would bend down and stroke him, and he would kiss my hand, always with this hard, warning stare, telling me to take no liberties, and if he did not intend to scratch at Madame McVey's door he would let me carry him up to the sofa outside my bedroom, and would kiss my hand again as I laid him down.

One autumn morning Madame McVey told me that he had not eaten at all the previous day, and later I looked out of my window at the grassy slope that drops from my house, and I saw under the branch of the great cedar a singular group. Gathered in a circle were Pounce, a large black and white cat which I had never seen before, two hen pheasants, and a cock pheasant. This is not so strange as it might appear. The pheasants in the woods round our house use our garden as a sanctuary, and they were so much larger than Pounce that he had always been on peaceable terms with them, though not so far as I had seen, in such close intimacy as this. Presently the pheasants whirred up into the tree, the black and white cat glided into the long grass, and Pounce came up the slope to the house. As he drew nearer I saw that his fur was harsh and the pride of his body had left him. When I picked him up he felt not quite a whole person, but like bones and muscles and flesh assembled within a pelt.

We sent for the vet, who could not come till the next day, and we tried to keep Pounce in the house, for it was cold. But he kept on escaping into the garden and curling up at one particular spot in a flower-bed, where the earth is banked up against the wall of the house; and we had to keep on bringing him back into the warmth. I was in the act of picking him out of the flower-bed when the vet drove up and I called to him, "This is the fifth time I have done this." He answered gravely, "That is a bad sign. They always seek a strange place to lie down, often quite an uncomfortable one, when they are going to die," and he took Pounce from me and began to feel his body for the lump which he was going to find very easily. When he had spoken the bad news, Pounce jumped out of his arms and walked towards me, staggering a little, but keeping on. We were back where we began. It was again as it had been when he was a kitten and tried to walk on the water among the nenuphars. He had shrunk, he looked quite small; and he had trusted himself to a surface that had looked as if it would bear his weight for ever, and now it was not keeping its promise, it was letting him fall through into a chill engulfing element. But he felt that all would not be lost, that nearly all would be saved, if he retained his dignity, and he tried to bear himself like a tiger.

At last I knew why my mother was frightened of cats. It was evidently not the same reason why Lord Roberts and Mr. Gubbins hate them. Cats can be depended upon to find an infinite number of ways of disconcerting human beings. But I did not doubt that my mother, always prophetic about me, had foreseen the state in which I found myself at that moment. But I had understood the warning thirteen years too late. This mattered, however, not at all, for she was wrong. The price I paid was enormous but I got full value for it.

[1] French film sex symbol of the 1950s

[2] French for "So-and-so"

THE NOVELIST'S VOICE

*Transcript of radio broadcast, BBC R*ADIO *4, Sept. 14, 1976*

W hen I wonder how I found my voice as a novelist, I am morti-
fied to find how little I can claim to possess such a thing as
a novelist's voice. I have published only five novels, and I
have been writing since my adolescence, and am now 83. But I know
that had I been able to do what I liked, and that is just what I have
not been able to do, I would have written nothing but novels. Fiction
and poetry are the only way one can stop time and give an account
of an experience and nail it down so that it lasts for ever. All other
forms of literature yield opinions and facts. But an account of what
one sees and hears and feels and tastes and the emotional judgements
of those sensory events, and the establishment of the relationship of
those findings to the rest of one's life; that one can only do in a novel
or a poem.

The exact rendering of experience was what I wanted to do from
an early age, because from the moment I looked around I was made
familiar with the uses of literature. There was a lot of the stuff lying
round my house. As a family, we had the advantage of reading very
quickly and remembering what we read, and the talk of our parents
joined on what we read to our lives. My father had the great advantage
of having as tutor a famous Frenchman, Élie Reclus, a geographer and

early vulgarisator of science, and ultimately a prominent figure at the Free University in Brussels. He had been engaged to teach my father and his brothers by their widowed mother, who met Reclus when he was an exile in Dublin. She was Anglo-Irish, and an impassioned member of the Protestant Established Church, which the English foisted on Catholic Ireland, and she assumed that any French person who was a refugee from France must be a Protestant in flight from the wicked Catholics. She was wrong. Reclus was an Anarchist and had gone into hiding because he and some friends had seized the Town Hall in the course of a rising against Napoleon III.

He accepted the post quite innocently, without any attempt to deceive, because she had told him she was a member of the Plymouth Brethren, and he had imagined that this was a small revolutionary body. When he discovered the truth he behaved with great correctness. He said nothing. He liked my grandmother, he liked her sons, and he thought he could teach them better than the next man, and he made it a rule never to recommend to them any idea of which their mother might disapprove; and there was forged a bond between them which never broke. My father used to tell the story with a chuckle, which became to me the sign of his appreciation of the random nature of human life, and the queer ways human beings counter it and impose a kind of order. Out of bigotry my grandmother had engaged the best possible kind of tutor for her sons, in fact the tutor most likely to prevent them from growing up bigots themselves.

This anecdote still rings in my ears and so does an anecdote my mother used to tell. She had in her youth been courted by a man so rich that his name was used over quite a large area as a symbol of riches. They went on a picnic-party, there he proposed to her, and she accepted him. But on the way home he realised that he had left his umbrella on the site of the picnic, and made such a fuss, was so seriously grieved, that she realised that he was not the husband she wanted, and the next day she broke off the engagement. What was valuable in this story was her candour about her emotions and her refusal to let it come to rest on a romantic falsity. Yes, she had rejected a philistine, but she wasn't, she owned, really a heroine. She saw that the thing would not do, but she was terribly disappointed, so disappointed that she shed a tear or two, because she was not going to enjoy unromantic and philistine security.

People were odd and they were complicated, and so complicated that however my father and mother's stories began one never knew how they were going to end, whether one would laugh or be sad, and life itself had that same unpredictable quality. Sometimes it turned out to be terrible. I had one relative who converted my childhood into pure panic whenever she managed to find herself alone with me. She was not a blood relation, she was the wife of my father's cousin, and far too often she came with an air of one about to distribute gifts, though all she gave was advice. I was frightened of her first of all because she was so large and I was so small, and though she had an immense bosom, she reminded me of a bull. It was partly her eyes, which were empty of anything but ferocity, and the way she held her head down and forward, as if about to charge. I always remembered her in later life, when my husband had a Jersey herd, and I used to help the vet with the T. B. inoculations, and one of our bulls was always nasty.

She used to get me alone, but she knew that my parents would have disapproved of her conversation. She always thought fit to remind me that my father had lost all his money, and that by his own fault, which was not strictly true, and that in consequence I would starve when I grew up unless I could earn my living, and this I would never be able to do, because I was so stupid, lazy, and for one reason or another, as unacceptable to the community as a leper. I very soon came to the conclusion that this was not the way a really nice lady would behave, and I used to find the excuse for leaving the room and resorting to the society of my sister Winifred, who was six years older than I was. She had a remarkable memory for verse and a beautiful voice, and it was her habit to soothe any irritation caused by such grown-ups as fairly could be classed in our language as rogue elephants, by reciting verse, Tennyson, or William Morris or Walter Raleigh or Wyatt or Marvell.

On either side the river lie
Long fields of barley and of rye[1]

she used to tell me; or again,

> *Give me my scallop-shell of quiet,*
> *My staff of faith to walk upon*[2]

Or again,

> *He hangs in shades the orange bright,*
> *Like golden lamps in a green night*[3]

Thus I discovered that personal sorrows could be relieved by a beautiful picture, which could be as vivid if it were written down on paper in words as if it were painted on canvas, and would be fixed in the memory, to be returned to for comfort or sheer pleasure. Later on, when I came to read Shakespeare at school, I learned that style could do more than that. I listened to my teachers and my fellow pupils and myself reading aloud from the poor immortal's words and turning them to dust, and I used to go home and ask my sister to read me the same passages, and at once the reason for Shakespeare's immortality struck on the ear. There was no doubt but that literature could do more than explain the random nature of life and the complications of human nature, it could abstract by the senses a knowledge of beautiful objects, and of objects not in themselves beautiful but seen with style, and make a powerful medicine of it. I take it that this apprehension does something to get one the voice of the novelist. It is equivalent to voice production.

In these ways I made a general approach to the lay-out of writing. But I found myself faced with certain difficulties due to my place in time. It means something that I write verse but write it with reluctance, and do not publish it. This is because I have never felt at ease with the poetry of my time. I have always felt at ease with the poetry of Raleigh, Wyatt, Donne, Marvell, George Herbert, and the love of poets who took on from them. I, God help me, grew up in an age when the Georgian poetry selected by Mr. Eddie Marsh, a secretary of Winston Churchill, was recommended to me. I turned with displeasure from this mush to Yeats and Hardy, and I may mention, as an example of the discouragement that falls to the young in the search for a voice, that my personal contact with my idols did nothing to help me because of the intrusion of the comic. Yeats was just like a foghorn. A foghorn on its own. He sat and hooted, and a fog materialised and closed in on him. And Hardy lived in a very ugly villa which he had built himself on the site of a Roman cemetery, and welcomed one by telling one how many bones they had dug up when making the drive; and one had a feeling that the awful little place ought to have a ghost-course as other houses have damp courses.

I couldn't go on with the new generation, largely because I found it impossible to take T. S. Eliot as the great man the Universities of the world have believed, and I still feel that if "Four Quartets" is a great religious poem, then all other religious poems have been worthless, and indeed all religious writers, including the authors of the Gospels. The result of all this is I keep my verse-writing to myself, I do not argue the point. I do not try to have a voice as a poet. Doubtless the consequence is that my verse is fossil verse. I knew a pianist once who decided to abandon performance but went on, in privacy, cultivating his art, all the more diligently because he now enjoyed perfect peace. He was kind enough to let me listen to him, and certainly he had become a marvellous player. But what I heard was fossil music. Sharing the artist's product with an audience does something to the artist.

In fact, I have not found my voice as a poet. But I have, I think, found my voice as a novelist. When I was in my late teens I met Ford Madox Hueffer, who was lying, worthless, and untrustworthy, but was loyal in his devotion to letters, and incapable of treachery to his standards; and I met his close companion Violet Hunt, a forgotten but admirable novelist, a kind and generous and lettered woman. Under their guidance I contemplated a changing fiction which had already, in the hands of Henry James and Joseph Conrad, claimed new rights. It was maintained that the novelist had a right to get as far away from plain narrative as a composer gets when he gives up writing piano solos and ventures on symphonies scored for the full orchestra. It was also determined to treat material of the highest seriousness. Joseph Conrad wrote of people who tried to do right in circumstances so alien and novel that the code they had learned in childhood had no immediately perceptible application; Henry James dealt with people who tried to do right but were confounded not by anything novel in their problems, but by the common acceptance of a code which decreed that the first duty of morality was to perpetuate the *status quo*.

At the precise moment when I came under the influence of Ford Madox Hueffer and Violet Hunt, they were helping a writer who had gone a stage further, and was wondering what was meant by "doing right," and speculating as to whether more importance should be given to the liberation of humanity from the repression of instinct by civilisation. This was D. H. Lawrence, and while I think he overstressed this problem, for the simple reason that he traveled so incessantly and had such brief and tempestuous friendships that he had no experience of ordinary long-term relationships and the operation of any settled community, he certainly improved fiction by representing human beings in their full passion and range. Both Henry James and Joseph Conrad drew characters as if they saw them through the wrong end of the telescope, as exiles are apt to see the natives of the land to which they are exiled. In any case, whatever was happening in the sphere of fiction, I was happy with it, I looked forward to writing novel after novel.

I was not to gratify this desire. For one thing I needed money. I had no capital behind me, and I had to meet heavy expenses, so I had to engage in journalism. I had to write articles, and this is death to novel writing. One has to write good articles if one is to capture the market, and this means shifting one's attention totally for the time being from any novel one may be writing, and it dries up the steady flow of the imagination. But I need not blame my need for money for my unfaithfulness to novel writing, for I had another and nobler reason for taking to journalism. After the First World War one had to notice that the world was changing. Heavens, how quickly, how drastically the world was changing. Can you blame me if I ran about the world watching it cast its own skin and put on the new? Can you wonder if I felt an urgent necessity to take an inventory of Yugoslavia, a country I loved, because I knew it was bound to be overrun either by Germany, or from Russia's direction by Communism; which would destroy its character, and blot out its inheritance from Byzantium? So I spent five years writing *Black Lamb and Grey Falcon*; and during the war I broke my knuckles on a brick wall protesting against the betrayal of Yugoslavia, which had not been a Communist country and had a Communist government forced on it by Great Britain and America.

And after the war I felt obliged to report the Nuremberg Trials, the Fascist-Communist riots in the East End of London, a lynching trial in a Southern State, a murder trial which happened in consequence of a system of trade controls, various treason trials. I think I should have been rather dumb-witted if I hadn't done these chores, and if I hadn't periodically visited the United States of America to see how one of the two Great World Powers was getting on with the business of preparing itself to guard the peace of the world. But I cannot fool myself that my spying journeys on the world made me the more able to write novels. I have indeed often come home from my travels with the conviction that quite soon people would not read novels because human beings would have forgotten how to read, as part of a general amnesia that would leave them with no memories except perhaps the technique for shooting arrows.

I was the more depressed because during this period fiction took a turn which I could not approve. I did not like modern poetry. I did not like current fiction because it seemed to me slipping into obsolescence. I admired without reservation the first two-thirds of Virginia Woolf's *Orlando*, but most of her other work seems to me mere gentility; a clutch at privilege on the ground of specially delicate perceptions. It seems to me sad that young people studying literature are regularly through the decades plied with *To the Lighthouse*, which is drawn-thread work. I have a feeling I am being slowly drawn back through time into the dim past. I cannot bear it that the young today seem to feel an affinity with writers who seem to me too old for my reading. If George Bernard Shaw were alive today he would be over a hundred years old; and Evelyn Waugh never in all his days let loose his satire on any subject that has not been mocked in *Punch* for the last seventy years. Graham Greene writes like Mauriac did forty years ago.

There was one novelist I greatly admired in the twenties and thirties: Henry Green. He was a truly original writer, his prose was fresh minted, he drove his bloodless scalpel inches deeper into the brain and heart, none of it had been said before. He is nearly forgotten. Now I admire Muriel Spark, for she is an innovator. And I am a fanatical admirer of A. L. Barker. If you cannot read her it is your fault. You should ask your vet to put you down if you do not admire *The Middling* or *An Occasion for Embarrassment*. I admire the grand architectural force of Paul Scott, and the subtlety of Francis King, notably his book *The Widow*.

Well, I am a warbler in the desert of fiction as I am an outcast from the small city of poetry. But it seems to me I have spoken three times with my own voice as a novelist. I think that I transmit my observations well enough in *The Thinking Reed*, a book about some rich people whose kind I used to know. I made my own sounds too in *The Fountain Overflows*, which was about children, and the differences between those who are born with a special aptitude and those who are not, and the cushions that good manners and affection can build to protect the losers from injury. It is half a book. I meant to write a sequel, or even two sequels. My personal life frustrated me. In one of the chapters in *The Fountain Overflows* I had to listen to a record of somebody playing the Mendelssohn Violin Concerto. It took me four days before I could hear it straight through. I had a house in the country; the oil for the central heating did not come; the doctor came to see my husband, the milk recorder came to check the yield of our cows, and so I suspected then I would never get the whole trilogy done. My suspicion was correct.[4]

But the novel in which I hear my own voice most clearly was *The Birds Fall Down*, which was published ten years ago. Its roots were planted in my mind over sixty years ago, by Ford Madox Ford[5], about a Russian police agent in the days of the Tsar, called Azeff, who really existed. He had the true Judas blood. He was not only a police agent, he was also a revolutionary, apparently with equal conviction, for he arranged assassinations of Tsarist dignitaries and officials on the one hand and the arrests of revolutionaries on the other with impartial vigour. The story had always attracted me, and one reason for my interest was that Ford Madox Ford had learned the story because he had met Azeff in London, had asked his sister, Juliet, who was married to a Russian exile, who the man was, and had been told of the suspicion which just then had grown up around him; and afterwards this suspicion was amply confirmed.

All this impressed me very much. Here in London the streets were orderly, the people seemed neat and sane. So, I was convinced, were most human beings all over the world. Amongst us had walked a monster, who betrayed comrades who trusted him, who used that treachery to kill people, some of whom he must have believed to be quite innocent, since they were picked from two parties who held opposing views. And Azeff went on doing it and doing it. That had a terrible consequence. The ploy had not in the end worked; the Tsardom had fallen and Azeff became an exile in Germany, was imprisoned, and released only to die miserably, and in all that hard time he can have had no excuse for himself. He just had no excuse. No man could be more destitute of an excuse to justify his sins, and no man can have had much blacker sins. But he must have pretended that he had an excuse, and sixty years later I wrote a novel, *The Birds Fall Down*, in which I looked for the excuse he had invented for himself. It is no use for me to try to give what that excuse was. Someone once said that if a poem was any good it could not be paraphrased, and it is as true that a novel cannot be condensed into a sentence unless it is a very bad one. All I can say is that he used a philosophical device to keep it from himself that he enjoyed treachery, that he was of the same blood as Judas. I feel that I spoke with my own voice as a novelist when I wrote that novel, because the peculiar property of a writer's voice is that it says things he did not know he knew till he heard himself saying them, and I constantly find myself giving information about the characters in the book which I think was valid, but which were fresh discoveries to me.

But literature, like all the arts, is the subject of quite arbitrary judgement. Who can say with confidence equal to that of a man announcing his measurements of a geometric shape that any writer of fiction speaks with the voice of a novelist? Some of the writers that speak to me with the recognisable voice of the novelist are forgotten. Once every five years or so I re-read two novels, which seem equally remarkable achievements. One is Thackeray's *Vanity Fair*. Everybody's heard of that. The other is *Caleb Williams*, by William Godwin, the philosophic radical whose political writings made a dent in the later eighteenth and early nineteenth century. Nobody's heard of that. Yet I find it a great book, a serious, eloquent, important book with a great subject: it deals with authority, the authority of parents, guardians, teachers, God the Father, and asks the question can God the Father be forgiven for the existence of pain, can anything be made of the superior-inferior relationship. And it finds a perfect myth, a perfect plot for this discussion. Why is it not a recognised classic? Such instances mean that the novelist, when he opens his mouth and speaks, has not the least idea if the proper voice for a novelist is going to come out. If he is absolutely sure, then it very often happens that he has not got a voice at all. The more intelligent a novelist is, the more he is aware of it. The more he needs faith: a secular version of the virtue, faith, celebrated by the theologians. A good novel cannot win honour on the information it gives: it cannot hope to be saved by its realism. It has to be a myth expressing real experience in terms that will stimulate the reader to regard experience in a new way. That is a larger order. Can it be done? One knows other people have done it. Can one do it oneself? Forget such questions and get on with the job. That, when we novelists open our mouths and give tongue, is what is in the front of our minds; and somehow, do you know, we like it.

[1] Alfred, Lord Tennyson, "The Lady of Shallot"

[2] Sir Walter Raleigh, "His Pilgrimage"

[3] Andrew Marvell, "Bermudas"

[4] West did, in fact, largely complete the trilogy: *This Real Night* (1984), and *Cousin Rosamund* (1985), the final, unfinished installment of the "Aubrey Trilogy," were published posthumously.

[5] Ford Madox Hueffer changed his name to Ford Madox Ford in 1919, after the end of WWI made his German name a liability.

Cortés Meets Montezuma

*An extract from Survivors in Mexico, with kind permission
from Yale University Press (orig. published 2003)*

Montezuma

The dilemma of Montezuma was uniquely acute. If Cortés and his men were mortals, then it was his duty to send his armies against them, and this he could do with not too heavy a heart. Even if the seers were right, and the pale invaders were fated to conquer the isthmus and destroy his Empire, the doom might take a long time to fall, according to the pattern of war the Aztecs knew. Each conflict began with prolonged negotiations setting out the issues between the two parties, went to a period of violent war lasting until one party or the other secured a positive advantage; and then the defeated party sought a temporary armistice which led to a peace conference as un-hurried as the preliminary proceedings. They had no inkling of total war, though a succession of the moderate wars they knew might be a warning of the period of catastrophe such as brought a Sun to its age.

But the accent of even these moderate wars was on the violence of the fighting that was sandwiched between the two periods of negotiation. If Montezuma went out against Cortés and his men, he had to deal out death with his slings and javelins and obsidian swords with all the power of his warrior nation. But what if Cortés was Quetzalcoatl returned? We can grasp Montezuma's position only if we imagine the British and American Governments of today faced with phenomena which might be either a hostile expeditionary force of space-men or the Second Coming of Christ. Even at that, Montezuma was in a state of conflict we would never know. He was a gentle man. Many speeches were recorded for us as they fell from the lips of this head of a ferocious state, hopelessly committed to ferocity; and they all speak of a wistful longing for a meeker dispensation. He must have hungered for that quality of mildness which is mysteriously implicit in everything we read of Quetzalcoatl. Yet he had been bred in a civilisation which conceived godhead as a raging and raving state, and the Plumed Serpent was coming back to drive out Smokey Mirror, who had dispossessed him. Montezuma must have feared his Christ for himself and his people as we could not fear ours.

Montezuma at once made an effort to find out whether Cortés was man or god by applying a very sensible test. He sent him, in the hands of the first party he sent to visit the invaders at San Juan de Ulúa, certain presents which he should have recognised, were he Quetzalcoatl. Among these were the head-dress worn by Smokey Mirror in his temple, which was made of feathers studded with gold stars, so voluminous that it fell about his shoulders as a cape; also the mask of Tlaloc, made of jewels and precious metals, and his standard; and a mitre of jaguar-fur attached to another of these splendid feather-capes; and a number of magnificent jewels of ritual significance. These last were most important of all, for it was believed that they had belonged to Quetzalcoatl, and indeed they may have been possessed by one of the men who called himself by that name. Cortés' acceptance of these gifts was debonair, for he had no notion that he was suspected of anything but humanity, and he saw in them simply confirmation of his joyful recognition that he was delivering over to the Spanish Crown a pearl among colonies. But it was as if candour was a principle that operated in him independently of his senses and his intelligence. He did not understand the question, but he gave the answer. He said, "What I want is gold," and there is no shorter sentence by which a man could prove once and for all that he was not a god.

Yet the message did not pass quite clearly from one culture to another. The demand for gold sounded slightly idiotic to the Aztecs, since it was to them not supremely valuable, but then this fitted in with the magic view of divinity as liking to talk nonsense and listen to it. But among the embassy Montezuma had sent a slave, not even a prisoner of war, a bought slave, a lout, disguised as the Governor of a province, and if Cortés had been Quetzalcoatl he would have seen through the deception. It seems that the chief of the embassy was at first fairly clear that he was dealing simply with men like himself, though differently coloured, but that situation shifted when he and his fellows noticed a gilt helmet worn by one of the Spanish soldiers: gilt and uncommon rusty, according to Bernal Díaz. They showed signs of awed interest and asked if they might borrow it and send it back to Montezuma, since it resembled a helmet which was worn by the god Blue-Hummingbird-to-the-South in his temple at Tenochtitlán, and which had come down to them from their ancestors of very long ago. (It is thought that this may have been another supposed possession of Quetzalcoatl.) Cortés kept a grave face as he acceded to the odd request and gave unwitting help to the hypothesis of his godhead by yielding to his trademark obsession and suggesting, with what seemed to his hearers divine dottiness, that the helmet might be filled with gold-dust when it was returned to him. The helmet swung back the balance, and it perhaps never came down on the right side again. Salvador de Madariaga, the best judge of this story by reason of his deep knowledge and his poetic imagination, thinks that the Aztecs never quite knew whether Cortés and his men were gods or not, and that Montezuma never ceased trying to resolve his doubts and may have been doubtful when he died.

Many of his efforts to find certainty were frustrated by the unhappy consequences of a liaison between an able intelligence corps and an army of highly trained performing magicians. The emperor was appalled by the sight of the helmet and also by the paintings brought him back by the artists he had sent to paint Cortés and his men, their armour and their arms, their interpreters, their horses and their dogs and their ships, which did indeed seem beyond the frontiers of heavenly and human affairs as he knew them. To test the competence of his magicians, he sent for a covey of wizards who lived on a lagoon at Chalco, Sweet Waters, which is near Tenochtitlán, reminded them of the prophecy of the conquest of Mexico by white men, and asked them how their studies had led them to picture these conquerors. Incautiously, they replied that the invaders had heads growing out of their chests and had only one foot apiece, so huge that they could lie down and shelter from the sun and rain under their soles. Montezuma then gave another covey its chance, a firm quartered at another lagoon, Xochomilco, the Field of Flowers. These had better relations with the Intelligence Corps, and they alleged that their studies had shown the invaders as white of face and body, long in beard, and clad in many colours, arriving on things that looked like mounds floating on the seas and, once they had landed, much given to riding animals that looked like deer but much bigger. This was only one example of the disadvantageous consequences for the client arising out of the magicians' tapping of security lines. It was correctly reported by Aztec spies that the Spaniards took special precautions in guarding their camps at night, which struck them as strange, since Indians fought by day alone. The magicians then had a revelation that the Spaniards were the children of the Sun and as such were invincible by day, but helpless by night. This led to a major defeat of an important Aztec allied force, which on these representations made a night attack. Nonetheless, magic had accumulated enough information about human behaviour for the Aztecs to have some very ingenious tricks at their command; and some of the best arose out of their technique of juggling with identities.

Montezuma's substitution of a slave for the Governor of the Province had scored a double success. Quetzalcoatl would have detected the imposture, as Jesus Christ knew that the woman of Samaria had had five husbands, though she told him she had had none; and, thus proved mortal, Cortés was revealed as wholly at sea in the society he was attacking, unable to tell a gross caste difference and therefore vulnerable. But Montezuma had another trick up his sleeve. When the second embassy arrived from Tenochtitlán, it brought with it a cartwheel of gold, engraved with a solar calendar, a cartwheel of silver engraved with a lunar calendar, and a great lord who was Cortés' double. It was explained that when Cortés' portrait had arrived at court the courtiers were all astonished at its resemblance to one of their own number; so they had sent the double along for Cortés to see him for himself. Again two purposes were served. In every Aztec temple it was the custom to choose priests bearing some likeness to the god who was patron of this particular pyramid and to emphasise the likeness by similarity of head-dress and cut of hair and pattern of paint on the face. If Quetzalcoatl were sent to a person who could be mistaken for him, he would recognise the priestly routine and approve; but if Cortés were plain Cortés, another end would be served. It appears that among the Aztecs, as among a number of Western people, a man who met his double felt terror and might even take it as a warning of imminent death. Presently, Cortés' double left, and the Spaniards were told that he had fallen sick. It was shortly after this that the embassy vanished in the night.

The episode misfired gloriously. When first the double arrived, the captains gathered round him and guffawed at nature's freakishness and called him "The Other Cortés" and then got on with entertaining the guests by a sort of non-stop gymkhana, galloping their horses along the sands and firing their guns and shooting their cross-bows and showing off their ships, and later they were distracted by increasing sulkiness about the shortage of food. There is no sign that Cortés or anybody else in the expeditionary force lost a moment's sleep over the *doppelgänger*. If Cortés had his uneasy nights, it was because he was under the strain of finding that a country he wished to annex for Spain by peaceful penetration meant to resist him, and that this country was so beautiful and strange that he did not want to make war on it and was also so horrible that, over an issue in which Spain played only a minor part, but which was vital to his own soul, he must break it and remake it. Also, no man wants to die before his time, and the supple Indian nature was twisting like a great snake in his hand. On his way to the capital and nerve-centre of this country, he would have to pick his way through these lying charmers who would offer him support which he did not dare refuse, but who would shift their allegiance as quickly as a snake can cast its skin. He understood perfectly that they had a right to betray him in their own interests, he was never fool enough to blame them for that, he knew he had no claim on their loyalty. Yet all the same he would have to punish them for resistance to this invalid claim, and that he hated, partly because of his eupeptic good nature, partly because of a professionalism which counted a killed Indian a failure, waste of one who should have lived to be a friendly and industrious colonial subject of the Spanish Crown. Neither Cortés nor Bernal Díaz write of enemy losses with exhilaration. The game they were playing was scored not like cricket but like golf, the object was to get round the course in as few strokes as possible. When the Spaniards came to the city of Cholula, where there was a temple for every day of the year and a parent temple which stood up like a mountain over the plains, it was discovered by Doña Marina that the Cholulans were planning to fall on them in the night; and the Spaniards had to destroy the great temple and kill six thousand people before they were allowed to go on their way. It is with regret that they chronicled the incident. They were pleased with themselves because they had avoided ambushes on the road, and they should have walked round this trap too. Such ambitions and economies, military and colonialist, were their preoccupations. But fate managed to link their straight paths with the winding trails, half on earth and half off it and never direct, of Montezuma's preoccupations.

About it and about these went. When Cortés started for Tenochtitlán, he left a small garrison near Vera Cruz. Quauhpopoca, an Aztec official in charge of a district nearby, was commissioned by the Aztec central authority to kidnap a Spanish soldier in order that he might be sent to the capital to be examined by the emperor for signs of deity, whatever those were. Quauhpopoca sent a message to the Spanish garrison telling them he had wished to visit them for the purpose of tendering his allegiance to them and asking for an escort of four men to see him through the territory of an unfriendly tribe. When the four men reached him, they were seized; two escaped back to the garrison, one was wounded, and one was killed. The killed and wounded men were bound to the backs of runners, but presently the wounded man died, and the runners found the grisly burdens insupportable, so cut off the heads and left the bodies by the roadside. When the heads were brought to Montezuma, he looked on them for a long time and grew pale, as well he might. One of the two had been a splendid young bull, with a great head and a strong black curling beard. The emperor decided that these were only men, but noted that they looked brave. With a characteristically sensitive and unimperial gesture, he ordered that the heads be taken away from the capital. He was for the minute free of his fear that Cortés was a god, but his heart was not in such doings. Then the scales trembled again when he heard of Cortés' visit to Cholula. Ironically, Cortés had been set on and nearly murdered by the dedicated worshippers of the god with whom he had been identified. The cult of Quetzalcoatl had its soul and being in that town. Now what was the emperor to think? The age was so committed to the belief that the worshipful was the disagreeable that Montezuma would find it natural for a god to celebrate his return by a massacre of the devotees. But would a god go so far as to overthrow his own great and glorious temple? The tests had to start all over again.

When the Spaniards marched down from the pass between the two volcanoes towards the Valley of Mexico, they found comfortable quarters in a caravanserai, one of the hostels for travelling merchants which were maintained all over the country, and when they had settled in they realised that the village round them was bubbling with a rumour that Montezuma was leaving his capital and coming along the road to greet them. And indeed an embassy did arrive before long, splendidly dressed, moving with ceremony, bearing presents which even by Aztec standards were munificent, and headed by an imposing figure who was treated by his suite with courtierly deference and who announced himself as the emperor, but who was not. It is said that this masquerade was designed to see whether Cortés, if he thought he had

Montezuma in his hands, would lay hands on him and keep him as a prisoner, in which case all the Spaniards would have been slaughtered forthwith. But this is improbable. Montezuma knew enough about Cortés through his spies and ambassadors to be sure that Cortés would have taken no such rash step on an unknown terrain, surrounded by enemies whose military resources he had not yet assessed. More likely, this impersonation was another sprat to catch a god. Only a divine intelligence would see through the disguise, it was presumed. Actually, Cortés, brought up in a household with some court connections, thought it incredible that a sovereign should be so careless of his dignity as to come so far from his capital to meet a foreigner.

Later the Aztecs told Sahagún a story, beautifully retold by Salvador de Madariaga, of the new folly to which Montezuma was inspired when the detected impostor returned. He sent out a posse of magicians to meet Cortés on the road and turn him back with their spells. While this party was still in sight of the capital, they met a peasant who was very drunk: possessed by Four Hundred Rabbits, as they would have put it, which was their Beatrix-Potterish name for drunkenness, for possession by the wine deity or deities. The magicians instantly recognised him and fell on their knees, at which the god made rude remarks about Montezuma and told them to turn round and look behind them at Tenochtitlán; and, obeying, they saw the towers and temples of their city going up in fire. It can be guessed that not only the peasant but the whole lot of them were drunk. There were stringent laws against drunkenness, which by a unique act of kindness to the aged was only permitted to old men and women, and even encouraged in them; but for public drunkenness a plebeian got beaten and had his head shaven if it were his first offence and was publicly strangled if it were not, while a noble would be strangled in private for even his first offence. But as it is extremely easy to brew beer and spirits from the cactus plants which grow everywhere, it can be guessed that the risk was frequently taken; and indeed there can never have been any time when a magician was more in need of a drink. One can imagine a furtive resort to a reed hut off the highway where there was a shebeen installed, some steady drinking in the company of a peasant who was against the government, and the unsteady emergence of several muzzy magicians out into the fresh air, and a sudden view of Tenochtitlán, which might well have been wavering and fusing even to sober eyes, for the prospect lay beyond land and water; and all of us have seen the glassy disorder which affects a distant object when looked at through an atmosphere striped with variations in temperature. When they got home with this hiccuping story, it filled the refined, the intelligent, the imaginative, the experienced Montezuma with gloom of the same kind raised in him by the most serious intimations of Cortés' genius. It is the special misfortune of the magic-eater that he loses his palate.

There was another and honest embassy sent to Cortés, with a message which demonstrates the Mesoamerican technique of negotiation: Montezuma warned Cortés that he should leave the capital if he had any regard for prudence and should return to Vera Cruz and leave the country, and that an Aztec mission would follow him with a tribute, which they would deliver to him on the sea coast, a tribute of great magnificence and quantity. Some authorities say that the offer was of an annual tribute, to be collected at a port. When Cortés' refusal was brought back to Montezuma, he held the last of many councils, which was on a sophisticated plane, spending much of its time on a discussion of the status of ambassadors. Then it sent on a final embassy a nephew of Montezuma, a young man of twenty-five, Prince Cacamatzin, the King of Texcoco, ruler of an adjoining territory on the lakeside. He arrived at Cortés' quarters on a litter that looked as if he were borne on branches, but the wood was jewel-studded gold and silver, and the foliage was made of green plumes, and he was carried by eight lords, who deferentially helped the young King to descend and swept the path he had to tread, but were said by the Indian onlookers to be the rulers of important towns. The King of Texcoco gave Cortés a warning of cold and courteous ferocity that he had better be gone, and Cortés offered him patronising assurances that the Spaniards would do him no harm, and he left in silent fury. Cortés and his men had been informed by their Indian allies, who knew nothing if they did not know the truth about the Aztecs, who were their masters, that Montezuma meant to let them enter the city and there would put them to death.

Tenochtitlán

In a daze, the Spaniards mounted their horses and rode out into the highway, which was crowded with sightseers, and presently they turned the flank of a little hill and for the first time looked on Tenochtitlán. Bernal Díaz has commemorated that moment: "When we beheld the many cities and towns settled on the water, and on the mainland, and saw the broad causeway running so straight and level across the lake to Tenochtitlán, we could liken it only to the enchanted scenes we had read of in the romance *Amadís de Gaula*, because of the great towers and the pyramids and the mansions that were rising from the water. Many of us asked if we were sleeping or waking. Never yet did man see, or hear, or dream of anything equal to that spectacle we saw that day." It is to be observed that these men of action were thoroughly literate. There is little descriptive writing, and that not very vivid, in *Amadís de Gaula*, but Bernal Díaz had read the book with his imagination as well as his intelligence.

Not insensitive, not brutish, he and his party went on, dazed with fear, dazed with beauty, until they were met by a party from the court, who took them to a lakeside town, where they were lodged in palaces built of stone and cedar-wood and hung with fine textiles and paintings and surrounded by gardens full of flowers and herbs and fruit-trees, laid round canals of clear water. In the morning they awoke and set out, still in a daze of admiration and fear, and found themselves walking across the great causeway over the lake, which was broad as two spears, and lined with people, for all of its three miles' length. The waters of the lake were now a solid mass of canoes. They were conscious as they walked that they numbered four hundred and fifty and that there were multitudes of Indians about them, and indeed they must have been surrounded by more than a million. As they walked, they observed that the causeway was broken at intervals by bridges which could be raised. They believed that the ruler of the city towards which they were going meant to kill them when they arrived, and they realised that the raising of a single one of these bridges would cut off their retreat. Bernal Díaz may be pardoned when he asks, "Now let who can tell it where are there men in this world other than ourselves who would have dared this danger?"

To read of their meeting with the emperor, it is best to turn again to the admirable Salvador de Madariaga, who synthesises all the reliable authorities. The Spaniards were halted just outside the entrance to the city, where an assembly of splendidly dressed Aztecs, numbering about a thousand, passed in turn before Cortés and performed the gesture which was apparently the standard greeting to the ambassador of an important power: each touched the ground at his feet with his hand and kissed it. Then the party was led through the entrance into the city fastness—the only entrance—and walked along more of that causeway, over other of those bridges, into a wide avenue between shining mansions and there saw advancing towards them two columns of Aztec lords, even more splendidly dressed than those who had paid homage, but all barefoot, keeping close to the mansions' fronts, leaving the roadway empty. They stopped, while a hush fell on the people who were looking down from the roofs, and down the empty space was carried the imperial litter, more glorious than the King of Texcoco's litter as an emperor is more glorious than a king. Before Montezuma could descend, it was necessary for the nobles to perform the ritual of sweeping the ground and covering it with cloths, and they had also to erect a canopy of green feathers hung with a fringe of dangling precious stones, and three heralds had to take up their stand with uplifted golden rods. Meanwhile, Cortés dismounted from his horse, and his men stood behind him in a trance. They had learned something of Aztec pomp from the royal embassies and the visit of the young king, but this was a greater glory. Díaz says with simplicity that the nobles they had seen before had changed into even better clothes; and indeed it is safe to think that when Montezuma stepped from the litter he was as magnificently attired as any human being since the beginning of time, for though the Indians had no silk, their feather fabrics took its place. He alone was shod, wearing high thick-soled boots like the cothurnus of the Greek tragic actors, but with the difference that the legs were encrusted with jewels and the soles were of gold. But this miracle of fantasy, this transmutation of a man and his clothes into a symbol of transcendent power, was seen only by Cortés and his men and the members of the royal house who stood under the canopy, for all others on the scene had their eyes fixed on the ground. Then Cortés advanced towards the emperor and there was a curious fumbling, which the onlookers could not quite understand, before a handshake was achieved, and Cortés threw about the emperor's neck a necklace, part of the supplied paste jewellery he had brought from Cuba to give to the natives on the assumption they would be savages, which he had tried to better by stringing it on a gold chain and scenting it with musk. After that, he opened his arms to the emperor in the embrace that was in Christendom the prescribed gesture between heads of state or their representatives but was frustrated by the two princes nearest the emperor, who caught him back in their arms to protect his sacred person from profane grasp. For they did not believe that Cortés was a god, they were sure that he was a man and as sure that he and all his company should be killed at once. Aztec society was so highly developed that it was not monolithic in its opinions, and those regarding religion ranged from absolute faith to scepticism. Probably nothing would have persuaded these minor kings and princes to abandon the faith of their fathers, both because their upbringing conditioned them to fear misfortune if they failed to propitiate the other world, and because their subjects might get out of hand were they not kept in order by sacerdotalism. But a joke is a joke, and they were not prepared to believe that a sweaty and travel-stained horseman (many of whose subordinates were known to have been killed in battle) was an immortal. When trouble brewed up later, they expressed their scepticism in words reported by the Spaniards, words reproaching Montezuma for the consequences of his bigoted faith and reliance on sorcery, which in spirit might have been uttered by contemporary liberals who found an elder relative committed to some reactionary political step by his fundamentalist faith. But Montezuma's power was still absolute, and as soon as all the nobles who had been standing with downcast eyes at the edge of the avenue had filed before Cortés and performed the act of greeting, he turned and led the way to the place where the strangers were to be lodged, walking with his hot-tempered young nephew, the King of Texcoco, while Cortés followed in the company of his brother Cuitlahuac, a signal honour, for he was nearly as sacred a person as the emperor. At a sign, a messenger came to the emperor and placed a packet in his hand. He bent over it for a moment and then turned back and threw over Cortés' head two necklaces of red shells, each hung with eight golden shrimps.

These were the insignia of Quetzalcoatl. The emperor had that morning received powerful confirmation of Cortés' deity. Cortés had been warned to turn back from Tenochtitlán for reasons of self-preservation that any mortal man would respect, and he had insisted on making the prohibited entry, on a day which by our reckoning was November the eighth, 1519, and according to one of the Aztec calendars the eighth day of the Month of the Wind, an ill-fated day, full of catastrophe and awkwardness, because it was under the sign of Quetzalcoatl, the Lord of Turbulence, of defeat, which somehow took precedence over triumph. A disconcerting aspect of this strange historical event is that the conclusion Montezuma drew from his superstitions was sounder than that of his rationalist relatives. It would have availed the Aztecs nothing to massacre Cortés and his men, for had he failed to return there were many other adventurers to persuade the Council of the Indies to sanction a larger expedition, which would certainly have been more cruel.

The palace set aside for the visitors was a former royal residence which had been for some time turned to use as a temple, a convent of priestesses, and the Royal Treasure House, and it was large enough to house not only the four hundred and fifty Spaniards but their two thousand native auxiliaries and their women cooks and camp-followers. Some rooms were so spacious that a hundred and fifty soldiers could sleep in one of them, each stretched out on the canopied sleeping-mat which was the Aztec form of bed; and there were gardens where they could wander, without feeling pent in. But this use of premises consecrated first to royalty and then to the gods must have been regarded as a profanation by all Aztecs not of the same mind as Montezuma, whose obsession showed itself again before the day was out. He left them before they were served with a dinner which Díaz, years afterwards, gratefully chronicled as "sumptuous." It probably deserved praise by any standards. The palace food was exquisitely cooked, kept hot at table on specially made earthenware vessels and eaten off the famous black and red pottery of Cholula. But when they had finished, the emperor was back with them and sat down and talked to Cortés in the presence of his companions. Now they had time to look at him, and he charmed them. He was a man of forty, slender and well-proportioned, with black hair and beard very elegantly cut, fine eyes, and an expression of good nature and cheerfulness, which was balanced by his gravity. It is apparent that he possessed the seductive Indian quality of cancelled voluptuousness, of strong sensuousness pruned back by an inner delicacy. He told them that he was happy to entertain them, because he knew quite well that they were travellers from the east whose coming had been prophesied for centuries. He was tactfully asking, "Are you Quetzalcoatl, come back from the place where the raft of serpents took you?" With perfect truthfulness, Cortés answered that he had indeed come from the East, and this plainly left Montezuma in an awkward position. He could not well ask him whether he was Quetzalcoatl or one of the mere men seen by the prophets, for fear of offending him if he were a god. He went on to make a hedging bet. He owned he had heard of the two lost expeditions of which Cortés had come in search and asked Cortés if all his soldiers were as brothers and were all the vassals of the same Emperor Charles. It may be suspected that not only was he interested in the two expeditions, but that his intelligence officers had reported to the near-mutiny there had been in Cortés' camp when some of his men had shown themselves partisans of his enemy Velazquez. Like all emperors, he thoroughly understood the principle of *divide et impera*, and so did Cortés, who assured him of the perfect amity of all Spaniards, which was the greatest lie he told in all the Conquest.

The next day, Cortés and his captains went to the imperial palace, into which, so like was Tenochtitlán to Venice, a boat could row, though it was in the heart of the city. This was a splendid edifice, not long built. It had twenty doors, three courtyards, many large halls, one hundred rooms, and not small ones, for the most part about thirty feet square, one hundred baths, fed by a water supply which was controlled by a beautiful fountain in one of the courtyards. The carpentry was superb: cedar and cypress, palm and pine were carved into ornate ceilings and furniture and doors, all dove-tailed, and the walls were of marble and porphyry and jasper and alabaster, and, where they were plain stone, they were hung with fine cottons, rabbit-hair cloth and feather-work. There was a great deal of decorative painting and wonderful carpets on the floors. Everything was exquisitely clean. The Spaniards held their breaths. Probably the only place in Spain where such luxury had been or ever was to be attained was the Caliphate of Cordoba in the tenth century, and there the scale was smaller; it is improbable that Cordoba had a population of more than half a million, while Tenochtitlán seems to have had its full million. Certainly not in the conquistadores' time had Spain had a ruler with such silken manners as Montezuma, who received the Spaniards in his private apartments, which normally only his family and his most important statesmen were permitted to enter, and who drew Cortés down to sit beside him on a dais, bidding the captains, with an air of being glad to have them there, find seats for themselves on the lower level of the room. The proceedings were watched by a party of Montezuma's relatives who, one imagines, had been addressing him on the beauties of scepticism and the necessity of keeping barbarians in their place, for Montezuma took a firmer stand. Cortés, not giving way for an instant to the convention that royal persons are allowed to choose the topics of conversation, at once launched upon the exposition of the Christian mysteries which he usually left to Father Olmedo. This is what he said, as it appeared to Bernal Díaz:

> He came to the emperor, he said, for the service of the Lord God whom the Christians adored, who was named Jesus Christ, and who suffered death for our sakes. He also explained to him that we adored the cross as the emblem of the crucifixion for our salvation, whereby the human race was redeemed, and that our

Lord on the third day rose, and is in heaven, and that
it is He who created heaven and earth and sea, and is
adored by us as Creator; but that those things which
he held to be gods were not such but devils, which are
very bad things, of evil countenances, and worse deeds;
and that he might judge how wicked they were, and
how little power they had, in as much as where ever
we placed crosses, they dare not show their faces. He
therefore requested that he would attend to what he
had told him, which was, that we were all brothers,
the children of Adam and Eve, and that as such, our
emperor lamenting the loss of souls in such numbers as
those which were brought by his idols into everlasting
flames, had sent us to apply an end to the worship of
these false gods.

Here Cortés stopped, for Montezuma was showing signs of impatience, and said in Spanish to his captains that he felt he had gone far
enough for a first interview and they could be considered as having
done their duty, and they rose to leave. But Montezuma put up a de-
taining hand. He cannot have been accustomed to having an audience
terminated by the persons he was receiving, and he had also to make
it plain where he stood.

"Malintzin, Mr. Marina," he said. "These arguments of yours are
already quite familiar to me. I understand that when you talked to my
ambassadors on the sand-dunes you put up a cross and kindly told
him about your three gods, and your party seems to have missed no
opportunity for spreading similar information during your journey
across my country. We have made no attempt to argue with you, because we have worshipped our gods for a long time and know them
to be good and just. So no doubt are yours. But please do not trouble
to raise this matter again."

Pleasantly he continued, "As to your great king, I am in his debt.
In other words, yes, I will pay tribute to him, I am ready to enter into
negotiations with you for a settlement."

The prudence he owed to his subjects here asserted itself. "As I told you before, I heard of those two parties of your kind of people who landed on the same coast as yourselves. I should like to know, are you all under the same ruler?"

In other words: are you worth negotiating with, have you the authority? Once more, Cortés assured him of the essential brotherhood of all Spaniards.

Then Montezuma's obsession seized him again. From the first he had wanted, he confided in them, to invite them to visit the cities of his empire and do them honour, and now the gods had granted him that desire, and here he had Cortés and his company all in his palace, which they must call their own and use as a place of refreshment and repose and never fear for their safety. If, he assured them, he had ever seemed reluctant to entertain them, it was not because of his own feelings, but because his subjects were frightened. And no wonder, for they had heard such terrifying stories about them. Why, he told them gaily, they had heard that the Spaniards carried thunder and lightning with them and discharged them when they wished, that their horses killed men, and it was even said that they were gods, and furious ones at that. But, he added, smiling at them as if they were long-known and much loved courtiers, he saw that they were men, simply men, though very valiant and wise ones. Doubtless there was a question-mark in his voice. The Spaniards beamed back at him, loyal as if they were his courtiers, and he turned laughing to Cortés.

"You know, people say such absurd things. Some of your Indian allies must have told you that I am a god and have nothing in my house but silver and gold and precious stones. But I'm sure you are too sensible to believe them. You've seen my palaces now and you can vouch for it, they're built of wood and stone, and look," he said, holding out his arms, "my body is made of flesh and blood. Like yours. I am a great king, and I have inherited the riches of my ancestors, but all the stories you have heard of my godhead and my bottomless fortune are lies."

He was asking two questions at once. Are you gods or men? And must you rob me?

But Cortés' Western ears could not hear the first question, and to the second he had the wrong answer, like all Europeans. Europe thought of itself in relation to the New World as a combination of missionary and entrepreneur, with a double duty to disperse the native populations' ignorance regarding Christianity and economics. The natives were certainly ignorant of Christianity, but it may be asked whether they did not know as much about economics as the next man. They had no monetary system, but they had evolved a rigid social structure, top-heavy with a large administrative class, where the civil service merged with the priesthood, and oppressive to the individual in its demands for taxes. This was all the economists of the admired Roman Empire had been able to produce, and it was not essentially different from what modern Europe has produced. The theory of the European invaders of the New World (insofar as they had a theory) was that they were conferring benefits on the native populations by inviting them to participate in international trade, and there they might have claimed to be genuine economic benefactors. But unfortunately they also felt compelled to confiscate both the accumulated wealth of the native populations and their natural resources, so far as these were mineral. This is not altogether the plain peculation that it appears, for they had an ingenuous belief that, as the native populations had no monetary system, these were wasted on them, and they were doing the only sensible thing if they took the minerals away and put them to useful purposes. It has to be remarked that these predators were actually conferring a huge benefit on another part of the world, on the Old World, by relieving its currency famine. This is not a moral universe.

It was no wonder that Cortés fell back on a compliment. "I do not expect to meet a more magnificent lord than you, not anywhere." He meant it, and he could not have spoken a truer word. He was to meet a lord not magnificent at all in his own emperor, that dreary Habsburg, who was to degrade his hereditary magnificence by his meanness; and indeed there have been few lords in all history as fine as Montezuma. Wherever he appears he leaves a sense of rich sweetness, like dark honey. Even the most ungrateful of routines he performed with a spontaneous yet not evanescent gravity, an ungrudging committal to pleasantness. At the end of this most unusual morning call he gave the Spaniards yet another present of gold and textiles, and they noted how handsomely he made the gift, seeming to delight in conferring a pleasure, showing no pang at all at the inroads on his wealth. They went back to their quarters talking of his gentle manners and his open hand and heart, and they decided to show him all the respect they could and never forget the courtesy of lifting their quilted casques in his presence. But the issue had been raised: between Montezuma and Cortés there had already flared up the one issue which was to sweep through this good feeling like a heath-fire and leave nothing but ashes, which was to break the heart of one of these great men and utterly destroy the other and his world.

The paradisal state of amity was to last four days. During this time the guests moved about their lodgings and grew more and more enchanted with the emperor and his works. His primary charm was a trait he shared with Cortés: both were specimens of an exuberant type, which they refined by their own innate artistic sense. Cortés was a conquistador who cut himself back and liked to eat to the sound of trumpets but eat little, was of an insatiable esurience but chose loyalty to the world of invisible things, which the senses cannot enjoy, who was greedy for vast estates but cared to cultivate them rather than exploit them. The Emperor Montezuma was the head of a great and unpliable state which imposed a florid magnificence on him and renounced its advantages to the self. The pomp with which he was surrounded was extraordinary by European standards. All who were received by him in audience, even the greatest nobles, had to strip themselves of their fine clothing and go into his presence in a plain habit and barefoot, to show they were as nothing compared to him. They could not even come in a straight line to his door, but had to approach it deviously. Yet the emperor made it plain that this respect was paid not to him but to his office. He treated all the Spaniards, of whatever rank, with a courtesy which stated that within his office was a human being of like flesh to theirs and, that flesh being perishable, they all owed each other kindness. They watched him as if he were not true. They were not homosexual, nor was the emperor, though the Aztecs were much given to homosexuality; yet they took much the same pleasure in him that they might have taken in an elegant woman who was also a good housewife. They liked the homely uses to which his fastidiousness turned the luxury, the cleanliness of his person and his garments. They admired the means he took to preserve his dignity, the screen which was set about him at the dinner-table so that no one should see him eating, the precautions taken to prevent it being known when he visited his harem of two wives and many high-born concubines. They enjoyed the playfulness which made him, in spite of his moderate appetite, amuse himself by visiting his kitchens and watching the cooks at work and smile benevolently on the singers and dancers and tumblers who came to perform when dinner was over. They were impressed by the quietness of the palace, the hermetic quality of the gardens and the parks, where there were canals and shady groves and flower-beds and theatres and picnic pavilions and an aviary and a zoo, which was also a temple, but never any bustle or display. Perhaps they would not have been sorry if they had been told that they were dead and this was paradise, and they could stay there for ever; and indeed it was much like a Moslem paradise, for they were even given lovely and well-mannered women.

But Cortés' inconvenient soul was stirring within him, and after four days he called together his three interpreters, Doña Marina and Aguilar and a page called Orteguilla, who had proved an apt student of the Nahuatl language, and sent them off to Montezuma with a request that he and his captains might be allowed to see the city. Montezuma immediately agreed, but his anxiety can be recognised in his decision that he himself should be their guide. Díaz records his own awareness that the emperor was apprehensive lest they should offer an insult to the Aztec gods in their temples; for that reason he would set aside his dignity and accompany them, to protect his gods, and also to protect them. The emperor's heart must have been heavy. The issue was to be openly stated, and emperors are used to preventing issues being stated that they wish to lie covert. But he had no choice. Cortés, who has come down through the centuries as the apotheosis of the amoral man, was faced with a moral decision, and he had decided it according to his standards of right and wrong, and that although he might pay for it with his life. Indeed, he had had other experiences on the way to Tenochtitlán than these which I have set down, which are all I knew before I went to Mexico, before I turned back to read the books. Why had I forgotten them? Because they represent a problem that my age ought to state and solve, that it refuses to state and has no prospect of solving.

Ever since Cortés and his troops had landed on the isthmus, they had found, wherever there was a town or a village of any size, large and well-constructed buildings of lime-washed stone, which were evidently temples, since there were altars and idols within. Their custodians were priests, not so different from the priests of Europe in their clothing, for they wore loose white robes like surplices or black hooded mantles like the Dominican habit; but they were conspicuously filthy, and their hair hung down to their waists or even their feet in twisted rats-tails clotted with blood, and blood dripped from lacerations in the lobes of their ears. There was blood on the walls and on the altars, but this did not come from the priests. There were always to be found on the premises some human bodies, their hearts cut out, and their legs and arms severed from their torsos. The sight revolted the Spaniards and more than the sight. There are those of us who have attended pagan sacrifices in parts of the world where only cocks and lambs and goats are offered up, and we know that the senses are sickened. Once, long ago, I drove up into the mountains on a pearly morning and got out of the car and looked through the clear air at a rock which shone red-brown. It was the altar of the sacrifice, and it was entirely covered with the blood of the beasts that had been slain on it during the night. As we got nearer, the stench of blood came and lived in our noses and throats like an infection. Later in the day, I was standing in a tavern in an upland village close by buying a bottle of wine, and suddenly the stench was with me again. Just behind me was the man who had stood on the rock and cut the throats of the victims, and the stench was in his clothes, massive as cloth itself. But there was more to offend than that. In the last moment of life, the goats and lambs voided their bladders and bowels, and so would men. But there was a further horror beyond the blood and the sewage. The joints were taken from the temples to the public markets, were hung up there to air, in Bernal Díaz' words, "as beef is in the towns of Castile" and sold for food.

THE CRAFT OF THE REVIEWER

[From typewritten manuscript, date unknown]

It is no use the reviewer trying to exercise his craft unless the organisation of the press provides him with conditions which enable him to do so. The first condition is that he must be given enough space for his reviews. This used to be the case in newspapers, but is no longer. When I started reviewing for the London newspapers in my teens, before the war, one was allowed twelve to fifteen hundred words for any book of the slightest importance. This enabled the reviewer to do his job: to state the subject of the book, to state what is its place in relation to the literature of its kind, to find out what individual contribution it makes, to subject it to criticism, to make it plain whether it will entertain the reader of average culture, or the reader of special interests, or nobody at all.

Then wartime conditions came to make paper a luxury, and those good conditions ceased. Reviews had to take their share in a general curtailment. Unfortunately, the human tendency to make a virtue of necessity got busy here, and editors began to declare that there was something substantially right in short articles and continue to this day to keep reviews down to a few hundred words. They developed a beautiful theory (doubtless based on Dean Inge's[1] astonishing belief that nearly the entire population of the United Kingdom is feeble-minded) that their public finds it difficult to keep their attention on any subject for more than two minutes and consequently has a passion for discontinuity as such.

When one suggests that there is strong evidence to the contrary in the fact that publishers find volumes of short stories much more difficult to sell than long novels, one is met by confused references to "modern rush," which somehow makes all the difference when it comes to reading the newspapers. Yet few of us spend only two minutes over our breakfasts, and nearly all of us spend many times two minutes in being transported from our homes to our work; and it is then that we read our newspapers. The proofs that this editorial attitude is nonsense are many. For one thing, since this system of potted reviews has come in no young reviewer has made a reputation. There is no reason to suppose that the stream of literary talent has run dry in that time; the more likely explanation is that the public finds it impossible to get in touch with even the most lively and ingenious minds when they are presented to it in snippet form.

For another thing, one no longer hears people saying, "Is the 'Brown Buttercup' any good? *The Daily* ------ says it is, but *The Evening* ------ says it isn't." They cite now only the weeklies or the longer articles in the Sunday papers. The sole exception to this is *The Evening Standard* because of its reviews by Mr. Arnold Bennett, who sensibly uses his position as top-dog to insist on being permitted to write a whole thousand words or so.

The reviewer's craft, then, can best be exercised on a weekly journal or in a privileged position on a Sunday newspaper. But even then there are conditions to be fulfilled before he can do his best. He must be in the lap of a good literary editor, who keeps in touch with the publishers' lists, who recognises his quality, and the type of books he can best handle, who cuts sensibly and does not think that the reviewer's idiosyncratic phrases must be slips of the pen because they are not clichés, who is moved by purely literary considerations and has no *arrière pensée* of an invitation to lunch with dear Lady B. that could be secured by a favourable review of her attempt at a novel, who sends the book out in good time, and who rewards worthy copy with appreciation. I count as the most perfect example of such an editor that I have yet encountered, Mr. Robert Lynd, the literary editor of *The Daily News*.

Writing for him was a blessing in other ways than the facilities he gave one by his kindness and his efficiency: for to know him and his work was to learn that if a personality was fine enough it could cultivate in the bickering turmoil of Fleet Street a fastidiousness, a leisurely but inexorable preference for fineness and dislike for baseness and cheapness, the kind of wit that does not surprise with a flash and go out into darkness, but that grows like a flower, such as optimists might hope to find in a college garden or a cathedral close. Such a personality states the problem (and announces that it can be solved) which continually faces all journalists and not least the reviewers: which is to withstand flurry, to cultivate in haste those qualities which ordinarily take time to establish and to maintain. It is something like the effort that most of us have to make when we are late for a train not to waste our energy by sitting in the taxi which takes us to the station with all our muscles tightened. How well Mr. Lynd solved this problem can be judged from the essays he contributed to *The New Statesman* over the initials T.T., which nine times out of ten are as unhurried as if he had to write one a year instead of one a week.

This quality, for which I find it difficult to find a name, since imperturbability suggests a lack of responsiveness to stimuli, a taking in with no giving out, which is the very antithesis of the ideal journalist's temperament, is one of a group of qualities that the reviewer must have if his work is not to be drudgery to himself and a bore to his readers. Some of these are almost in the nature of physical equipment. To begin with, the reviewer must be a quick reader, for it will often happen to him that important books are sent to him to be reviewed in two or three days, so that the notice can be printed on the day of the book's publication; and there is an indirect but no less powerful compulsion in the fact that most reviewers are not paid at a rate which enables him to spend a week or two digesting a single volume.

This is the only advantage I ever had as a reviewer. Last week I proved to the satisfaction of a friend that I can read a detective novel in an hour and a half, even such an elaborate one as *William Cook — Antique Dealer* or *The Marloe Mansions Murder*, and pass an examination on it afterwards without a mistake. I do not myself understand how it is done, as in the case of a book of sixty thousand words this involves over six hundred and fifty words a minute; but I have known many other people besides myself among reviewers who could do it. With more subtly written books the time taken must of course be longer; and I have never known a reviewer who did not regard it as a matter of conscience to give such time as the book demanded. I have never reviewed a book which I have not read from cover to cover, and I would not mind standing bail that almost every reviewer that I know could make a similar declaration.

To be a quick writer is equally an advantage, but of that I, who am a slow and nervous writer, who cannot fix on a beginning, who tear up my copy again and again, have no personal experience. I have, however, been privileged to admire Mr. Ford Madox Ford when I have seen him write straight on to the typewriter in something less than two hours a beautifully thought and expressed article of two thousand words, so I can have no illusions that easy writing makes hard reading and *vice versa*. There is here, as in the matter of reading, simply an enormous difference in individual physical and psychological ways of performing an act which has no bearing on the value of the result. Quick writing brings the same practical advantages as quick reading, and is not so important as the possession of a good memory, which will enable the reviewer to follow up the references in the book he has been dealing with and see just what facts in letters and life illuminate it or are illuminated by it. I have never known a reviewer more magnificently endowed in this respect than Mr. S. K. Ratcliffe. It is a joy to see how he can take up a book on any branch of social history and bring forward every political event of the last hundred years and every passage from great and middling writers which are made more important or less so by its arguments and findings of his immediate subject. The scholarship of Virginia Woolf gives us again and again the same delight in *The Common Reader*.

This quality, which is more than mere memory, which is memory combined with an eye for what according to the highest scale of values are true relationships within reality, need not be accompanied by such grace of writing as in Mrs. Woolf's pages. I came across a striking example of that the other day on the back of a press cutting that was sent me from America. There a journalist who had no sort of gift for turning a sentence and finding an expressive phrase had been given a tedious enough book of memories by a musician to review, but the result of this unpromising combination was brilliantly interesting because he had had enough of this something more than memory to make him plough through the gentleman's boastings about minor royalties who had nodded their heads in time to his valses and his account of a visit he had paid in his childhood to Courtavenel, the home of Pauline Viardot-Garcia, the singer. Turgenev is casually mentioned as being one of the guests staying in the house: but the reviewer remembered that it was with Pauline Viardot-Garcia and her husband that Turgenev lived for over thirty years, in an intimacy that puzzled and sometimes scandalised the society of their time. This was, in effect, Turgenev's home.

The reviewer seized on various significant details that brought before one the social atmosphere of the place, and pointed out how very natural it was that Dostoevsky, who suffered agonies because he had been thrice exiled from his beloved Russia, once to Siberia by the Tsar, once to the highways and byways of Europe by his importunate creditors, should never be able to come to an understanding with Turgenev, who voluntarily left Russia to live in French drawing-rooms, where opera singers' children played very agreeable charades. With a few intelligent comments he made a dull and unimportant book add to the interest and importance of Dostoevsky's *The Possessed* and his letters. I call that journalist a reviewer who really knows his craft.

These qualities—quickness of assimilation, quickness of expression, a selective use of the memory—can only be released by a more fundamental quality, which is the capacity for day in and day out keeping up a lively interest in the universe, and rushing at every new phenomenon that presents itself (such as a new book) as hopefully as a puppy rushes to the front door every time a new visitor enters. If a reviewer has not this attitude to life, he is apt to sink into its contrary and regard every fresh book sourly as a nuisance. The reviewer who is ideally equipped in this respect (though he now reviews plays more often than he does books these days, but there is little difference in the fundamental qualities needed for these two occupations) is Mr. St. John Ervine. The other day I was at a party where a misguided host engaged for the delectation of his guests a female of repellent aspect who, in a voice naked of charm, sang songs announcing her own immoralities (in which I found it impossible to believe unless it is profoundly true that Englishmen take their pleasures sadly) with the baldness of Bradshaw. My grief at her performance was assuaged by the sight of Mr. St. John Ervine's face across the room. Convulsed with the same emotions I was experiencing, he was nevertheless watching her performance with a bright-eyed scrupulous attention, placing her in regard to similar performers, evaluating her technique, extracting her essence, passionately interested in her because she was alive. It is because he is perpetually actuated by such a spirit that one turns to his page in *The Observer* every Sunday.

The trouble about the reviewer's craft is that once the craftsman has learned it there is no certainty that he can go on exercising it for any great length of time. A writer who has sufficient power to write interesting reviews usually comes to a point when he wants to indulge in creative work on his own account, and if economic conditions or habit keep him to writing reviews after this time his interest is apt to flag and he may even feel resentment against the writer whose books he is dealing with, since they have had the luck to get on with their creative work and thereby are now keeping him from his. The effects of this attitude are sometimes to be seen in a general flatness of style and spirit and more regrettably in a tendency to praise second-rate work at the expense of first-rate original work. This is usually done in all sincerity; conscious malice is rare in reviewing. Hence, the best reviews are done either by young writers or by people whose temptations preserve them from this temptation: by people whose creative talent would naturally take the essay form and thus can remain both critics and creators, like Mr. Robert Lynd and Mr. T.S. Eliot; by people of exceptional vitality who can turn from reviews to the writing of books as Mr. St. John Ervine and Mrs. Woolf do; and by people who for some reason are inhibited from developing their creative side, although they have it. The most conspicuous example of this is Mr. Edmund Gosse, whose masterpiece *Father and Son* explained why he never wrote another; a child so rigidly suppressed, so wrapped in negative suggestions from its birth, would be unlikely to bring to adult life the power to make those series of self-assertions which result in creation. There are enough reviewers of these several sorts to make the author feel confident that somewhere or other in the press, and perhaps even in the bulk of the press, his book will get fair treatment; and to make the public confident that the best of literature is not going past them unreported; which is to say that the craft of reviewing is not in decline in England at the present day.

[1] William Ralph Inge (1860-1954), Anglican priest and Dean of St. Paul's Cathedral in London, scholar of neoplatonism and advocate of eugenics.

Reviews

AREN'T MEN BEASTS

A review of PATRIARCHAL ATTITUDES: WOMEN IN SOCIETY *by Eva Figes,*
THE SUNDAY TELEGRAPH, *June 28, 1970*

There is, of course, no reason for the existence of the male sex except that one sometimes needs help in moving the piano. How wrong males are, how unfit they are for any part in this universe (and possibly in any parallel universe either) was shown this summer in the South African cricket tour fuss.

Cricket is only a game. One set of males throw a ball about, others take turns in hitting it with a piece of wood, the males change roles, they slowly walk about. It cannot possibly matter, in any real sense, whether that ball is or is not hit by that piece of wood. Why insist on this non-event taking place if there was a possibility that it would cause any sort of trouble?

And why should it have caused any trouble? Only because there were more males about, pretending that if they stopped the game it would be a protest against the South African policy of apartheid. But from first to last, no attempt was made to prove that any of the South African team supported apartheid, so harassment of them may have been as idiotic as beating a Tory M.P. for a misdeed committed by the Labour Government.[1]

The incident was so gross a demonstration of male defect that the obvious thing, with the general election looming up soon after, was to start an agitation to deprive men of the Parliamentary vote. But men do not excite censoriousness; and that is one of the most important differences between the sexes.

For women, as Eva Figes shows in *Patriarchal Attitudes,* provoke censoriousness no end. Mrs. Figes has gathered a notable sheaf of quotations from the great didactics, beginning with Rousseau and coming to a climax with Freud, all looking at the opposite sex as if they had seen a ghost, turning white as a sheet, crying out that this is against nature, and working out rites of exorcism by restrictive conventions.

Even Darwin, whom one had thought of as a calm scientist, shakes like a leaf and makes the most astonishing allegations. According to him, the feminine virtues, though winning, are those found among "the lower races" and were survivals of past and inferior civilisations embedded in the species. My love is like a red, red rose and is also a fossilised Neanderthal.

Darwin ventured on an apothegm, not daring in itself, which it was nevertheless daring of a masculinist to attempt. "No one will dispute that the bull differs in disposition from the cow." The male had better be quiet about that.

The bull discharges a necessary function but makes an unnecessary fuss about it. He spends his life enjoying agreeable relationships with the female of his species (brief, it is true, but he has no basis for comparison), with all found, and is asked for nothing more. Why does he bellow, paw the ground, chase harmless ramblers into hedges, and seek to toss them on his horns in a frenzy of biologically useless rage?

If women were as censorious about men as men are about women, they would have something to say about the bull, whose case arouses various questions, such as why Napoleon did not stop fighting when he had consolidated the French Republic, and what about that extra male chromosome which makes the criminal.[2]

But really, what a pack these masculinists are. Mrs. Figes exhumes for our benefit W. E. H. Lecky, the 19th century historian, who was of the opinion that the prostitute was "ultimately the most efficient guardian of virtue. But for her the unchallenged purity of countless happy homes would be polluted." And she has unearthed an even more painful quotation from this old humbug:

"There are always multitudes who, in the period of their lives when their passions are most strong, are incapable of supporting children in their own social rank, and who would therefore injure society by marrying into it, but are nevertheless perfectly capable of securing an honourable career for their illegitimate children in the lower social sphere to which these would naturally belong."

Molière could have used this sentence as it stands in *Tartuffe*, and sickening it is in its evocation of carefully kept account books and seduced housemaids.

But stuff as sickening has been written far nearer to our own time by others, including Sigmund Freud. It is curious that psychoanalysis, which has had such an immense influence on the 20th century, has injected Anglo-Saxon culture with the mores of 19th century Jewish Vienna.

Freud, who would be 114 were he alive today, grew up in a stable economy which enabled Jewish households to support all their women-kind in comfortable homes with no other duty except to pamper their husbands and be pampered in the cosy traditions of their people.

When he went into psychiatric practice in the last decades of the 19th century, he found that many of his women patients had developed other ideas and wished to use their brains and perhaps earn their own livings. This shocked him deeply, and he tried to rectify the situation by analysis, a theory which many patients encountered with amazement and which, here restated by Mrs. Figes, still seems amazing.

Freud preached that all little girls felt deprived and envious because they had not the same sexual organs as the male. When it was objected that many little girls knew nothing about the male sexual organs, he claimed that there was a bush telegraph in the unconscious which carried the news to the little girls.

Once Freud and his disciples got a female on the analysis couch and found traces of intellectual activity, they attempted to persuade her that she had prolonged the alleged little girl's alleged dream into adult life and was seeking in work a substitute for the male sexual organ.

When the female patients refused to accept all this nonsense, Freud and his disciples tied up the argument nicely on their side by calling the refusal psychical rigidity.

The question arises whether the human race has ever been as silly as it has become in our time. It adds a wild charm to the scene that of course the female patients were paying large fees for this depressant rough-housing.

Patriarchal Attitudes is perhaps more valuable as an anthology of masculinist excess than for Mrs. Figes's own theories, which would appear to better advantage if they were developed in a separate volume. As it is, she seems to show undue pessimism about the possibility of men and women living in the same world. A bull may be noisy and dangerous, but it is not impossible to keep one.

Among the incidental material, there is recorded the interesting fact that Mrs. Beatrice Webb declared at a public luncheon that she had never met a man, however inferior, "whom I do not consider to be my superior." She was, of course, speaking the truth. She was inferior to any man she met, and any woman, too, because, brilliant, clever, and fortunate, she was capable of making that statement without believing it, in order to increase her attraction and influence.

It is also interesting to note that Rousseau apparently did not know who Ninon de l'Enclos[3] was. He wrote of a bluestocking: "From the lofty heights of her genius, she scorns every womanly duty and she is always trying to make a man of herself after the fashion of Mademoiselle de l'Enclos."

This is not what Ninon was doing, when last heard of.

---

[1] Apartheid (meaning *separateness* in Afrikaans) was a system of legal racial segregation enforced by the National Party government of south Africa between 1948 and 1990. Although it seemed ineffectual at the time, the ban on South African participation in international sporting events was frustrating for many whites in South Africa and is widely credited with being partly responsible for forcing the country's abandonment of apartheid.

[2] An extra copy of the Y chromosome is associated with increased stature and an increased incidence of learning problems in some boys and men. When chromosome surveys were done in the mid-1960s in British secure hospitals for the developmentally disabled, a higher than expected number of patients were found to have an extra Y

chromosome. The patients were mischaracterized as aggressive and criminal, so that for a while an extra Y chromosome was believed to predispose a boy to antisocial behavior (and was dubbed the "criminal karyotype"). Subsequently, in 1968, in Scotland, the only ever comprehensive nationwide chromosome survey of prisons found no over-representation of XYY men, and later studies found XYY boys and men had the same rate of criminal convictions as XY boys and men of equal intelligence. Thus, the "criminal karyotype" concept is inaccurate and obsolete.

[3] Ninon de l'Enclos was a 17th century author, courtesan, and patron of the arts, commemorated in Dorothy Parker's poem "Ninon De Lenclos, On Her Last Birthday."

THE GREEK WAY

THE CHALLENGE OF THE GREEKS, by T.R. Glover,
SUNDAY TIMES, Aug. 23, 1942

For some occult reason, the story of the relations between the Early Church and the Roman Empire is told in our schools almost exclusively from the lions' point of view. This encourages masochism in the young and is not in consonance with the facts, which present us with a picture of a brilliant and sensitive and audacious group of Christians, stimulated to the point of inspiration by the new ideas of their teachers, taking over power from the limp hands of pagans who were perishing because their minds were growing on exhausted soil. That story, and the story of a time extraordinarily like ours, a cruel and terrible time testing the spirit in a thousand ways, is delightfully told in a book by Dr. T. R. Glover called *Life and Letters in the Fourth Century,* which was published forty years ago but should not be forgotten. It makes very good reading today. The analogy with our own times is cheering, though it is an analogy between grief and grief, because we are here to see it. The fourth century looked like the end. It was a beginning.

To many, the name T. R. Glover on a cover must recall that book, but he has written forty others. He is an indefatigable populariser of the classics. The volume he has just published, *The Challenge of the Greeks,* is particularly interesting to women, for a certain peculiar reason. To be born a female brings upon one many curious and interesting experiences, among the less publicised of which is the asymmetrical system of classical education prevalent in girls' schools. Many English and Scottish schoolgirls study Latin nearly or quite as industriously as their brothers, but are taught no Greek at all.

In *The Challenge of the Greeks*, Dr. Glover tells us, in one essay, just what we have missed in not learning Greek, and in another how people ought to be taught Greek to get the best out of it, and in another what is the essential contrast between the Greek and the English way of conducting life. The docile ignoramus in search of instruction from initiates is bound to think that these essays are just what he, or more probably she, wants. But there are far more slips between pen and reader's sympathy than there ever were between cup and lip; and though other essays in the volume bring back the hankering for a full classical education, these particular ones, designed for that purpose, in fact repel it.

They raise the shocked surprise we so often feel when scholars, after showing the most delicate perceptions, the most infallible taste, show actual dullness of palate when they sample the real life around them. In a rumbling admonitory style, not sufficiently precise, Dr. Glover alleges that we should study ancient Greece because the Greeks were highly individualised, and our modern world is standardised to the point of soulless monotony. "We go," says Dr. Glover, "to schools of one type; we read newspapers of one type; as for books, we read best-sellers or none…" A complaint ought to be a little truer. Do we all go to schools of one type? The admirable schoolmistress in my own village, as well as netting a nice lot of scholarships, teaches her pupils to sing "the sailor with the navy blue eyes[1]." She rightly feels that, as they are going to sing this in any case, they had better sing it well. This is not done at Winchester or Roedean. Many such sensible adaptations of the educational system have come my way, and I have not searched for them. And surely nobody could mistake one of our newspapers for another, though an error of another sort has been known to arise in connection with them. In the days when newspapers were vast and voluminous, an American millionairess, on her first visit to London and anxious to understand England, set herself every morning to read the great newspaper, from which, she was told, such understanding could slowly but surely be distilled. Partly owing to its sedate method of presenting the news and partly owing to the nobly resistant style of the leaders, she never realized till the end of the week that she had been reading the same copy over and over again. And do we all read best-sellers? The angry reader will find sentence after sentence like this, which is mere grumbling.

These essays are full of like disputable points, which arouse the reader's profoundest resistance. It will seem dubious whether the Greeks were so individualised. After all, according to Plato, Socrates had the most astonishing luck in always making everybody he met say what he wanted. They always asked him the right question, never made the interruption which would have ruffled his argument. Athens must have been a city of stooges, of philosophical Dr. Watsons. We find ourselves suspecting the Hellenists of having the same grounds for their enthusiasm as Hegelians, who, it is said by the ribald, undergo such pain and toil in reading Hegel that they cannot bear to admit at the end that they have wasted all their time and energy on studying false doctrine and have to become adherents of his philosophy.

But then one comes on other essays in which Dr. Glover writes of ancient Greece without falsely rationalizing his enjoyment, in which he rummages in his store of knowledge and turns out scraps he loves for considerations other than their moral elevation: essays in which he tells how the Greek treated the forest, how he farmed, how he victualled hungrily situated Athens, how he traded. And there it is about one: Greece, ancient Greece, in which, as the scholar Humfry Payne put it, "there was an animate existence lifted up, freed from grossness and decay by some action taken by the mind, which the rest of the world cannot practise." This is, like Dr. Glover's earlier book, *Life and Letters in the Fourth Century,* a heartening book. That told of a day that looked like the end and was a beginning. This tells of a world so magical that it might be created again, any time, for no reason apparent to man.

[1] A popular WWII song by Al Hoffman, Victor Mizzy and Irv Taylor
"Who's got girls in every port
Hanging around like flies
Yo-ho-ho-ho-ho-ho
The sailor with the navy blue eyes"

TELLING HORATIO ABOUT IT: POPULARISED PHILOSOPHY

A review of THIS IS MY PHILOSOPHY, *edited by Whit Burnett,*
SUNDAY TIMES, *May 25, 1958*

Among the many reasons we have for respecting Shakespeare, there should be placed high his provision of a sentence which meets the need of anybody who, in whatever circumstances, wishes to be mildly offensive to a fellow-creature without putting himself to too much trouble. "There are more things in heaven and earth, Horatio, than are dreamt of in your philosophy." It has been worked to death, of course, and is now rarely used except in minor detective stories, where sub-Holmeses employ it to crunch sub-Watsons.

Nevertheless, it is the perfect instrument for its purpose. There is the padding solemnity of the first line, which sounds as if the speaker were some large and dignified animal going slowly and prudently about its business; and the ungainly hurry of the second line, which suggests a smaller, trivial and incompetent organism, say, a clumsy dancing mouse. There are the implied statements that there is something to be known and that the person addressed does not know it, and that the speaker does know it, and the magnificent abstinence from any revelation of what it is that is known. It is to be remarked that Hamlet did not go on to explain to Horatio the place of ghosts in the cosmogony; he said, "But come," and changed the subject. This precedent has often been followed.

This contribution to the dialogue of offence is sometimes brought to mind by the anthology of contemporary philosophical writing, *This Is My Philosophy*, which has been edited by Mr. Whit Burnett, an American skilled at such works of popularisation. The volume shows philosophy at its least technical and satisfies only the loosest definitions of philosophy, say, as the science of principles, or the art of considering the part in relation to the whole, and sometimes even recalls the use of the word in Martin Tupper's "Proverbial Philosophy.[1]"

Such are the overtones of our language that the sub-title, "Twenty of the World's Outstanding Thinkers Reveal the Deepest Meaning they have Found in Life," conveys to the experienced that this is just what the twenty authors involved do not do. What has happened is that the editor has chosen from the works of each something which he thinks the average man will be able to understand. This is, in fact, an attempt to bring Horatio into the conversation on more civil terms.

The contributors can be divided into two groups. One consists of Bertrand Russell, Lewis Mumford, J. B. S. Haldane, Albert Schweitzer, Aldous Huxley, G. M. Trevelyan, C. Jung, and others that weigh in at an average age of seventy-four; and the other group consists of Robert Oppenheimer, Jean-Paul Sartre, Ignazio Silone, and Werner Heisenberg, the director of the Max Planck Institute for Physical Research, whose average age is fifty-three.

Most interesting of all contributions by either group are four expositions of Christian philosophy. One is an article by Reinhold Niebuhr, sombre and solid, which suggests just what apparently reasonable concepts Christian philosophers think have to be scrapped if the part which is the life of man is to be fitted into the whole which is the universe, and what case there is for regarding the concepts which have to be substituted as more reasonable. This is clear thinking which the most sceptical must respect; it is, in fact, the thinking of a man trained in the technical philosophy hardly represented in this volume. There is also an impressive article by the octogenarian Professor Hocking which takes us back into the past, when the religious saw the modern scientists coming towards them from the horizon and realised that they were bearing gifts of new truths but were often hostile to the old truths.

He quotes a key passage from that impressive little book which was written in 1879 by Gustav Theodor Fechner, the physicist and psychologist, *The Day-View in Contrast to the Night-View*, in which he (a fervent deistic pantheist) expressed the dread that materialism was going to drive joy out of human experience. This seems absurd to us: who, if we were asked by some fairy-tale king to find him a happy man, would talk no nonsense about shirts, but would tell him to turn on his TV set and wait for Dr. Bronowski.[2]

But Professor Hocking's article shows how necessary it was, in order to preserve the threatened joy, to capitulate neither to old bigotry nor to new, and to maintain the tradition of philosophical argument. For we are, as Professor Karl Jaspers shows in his article, often in danger of being injured by materialist philosophy not because it is materialist but because it is bad philosophy. Professor Jaspers is a Christian existentialist, but as one watches the welter of whirling arms and legs in the dialectical fight no one could guess which participant was on the side of meekness.

There is one great fault in this volume. The Christian philosophers and scientists are constantly accusing each other of inability to think; and many of the essays written on behalf of science bear out that accusation. There are some fine examples of the dialectic process which might be termed "the dying pig." "If we are ever to control our evolution," writes J. B. S. Haldane confidently, "we shall certainly have to overhaul the whole mating system." This sounds quite an enjoyable project, but he weakens. "By this," he adds, "I do not mean that we shall have to abolish marriage or adopt polygamy." He weakens still farther. "I do not know what we shall have to do," poor Mr. Haldane ends. The pig is dead. But it must be remembered that Mr. Haldane is not only a scientist, but took a first in Greats. Whose fault is it if he cannot think? Not science's.

There is, moreover, cause for irritation in the contribution made to this volume by an acclaimed French Christian philosopher, Monsieur Jacques Maritain. Here, as in his other writings, he flies the flag of adherence to the philosophical system invented by St. Thomas Aquinas, one of the noblest products of the human mind.

What gives pain is that his writings, except when they specifically expound that system, often show few signs of its influence. They follow a current of liberal religious thought which is part of the prevailing European tide; it is as if *"The Tablet,*[3]*"* wishing to be on good terms with all manifestations of the Zeitgeist, kissed its hand to *The New Statesman.* His contribution to this volume begins with the usual proclamation that he will never desert St. Thomas Aquinas, but it ends in a discussion of the Christian attitude to social problems which might have been written by Frederick Denison Maurice or Scott Holland or Stewart Headlam, or any other of our old Christian Socialists: excellent men, but not noticeably Thomists.[4]

The allegation that all the imperfect thinking is on one or other side of the fence really does not hold water. It is true that Mr. Aldous Huxley makes on behalf of science a painfully rash claim that to meet the problem of over-population the world should place its resources under an international control which shall be a "primarily technological alliance." But Mr. Huxley is, in fact, not a scientist. Mr. J. B. S. Haldane is a scientist, and can certainly think on his own subject of genetics, but he confesses again and again in his article that scientists at present lack the information which would enable them to take the responsibility of shaping life. Professor Niebuhr quotes with loathing a scientist, Alexis Carrel, who felt no such humility, and wanted a body of scientists to spend twenty-five years studying anatomy, physics, physiology, metaphysics, pathology, chemistry, psychology, medicine, genetics, nutrition, pedagogy, aesthetics, ethics, religion, sociology, and economics, and then at the age of around fifty address themselves "to the reconstruction of human beings." But surely Alexis

Carrel was a Christian?

In fact, the division between scientists and non-scientists is nothing like as clear-cut as is pretended; and it is not surprising that the contributions made by the two scientists in the junior group, Robert Oppenheimer and Werner Heisenberg, who accept the existence of this division, though they want to end it, are unimpressive. The other two, Silone and Sartre, are more interesting if only because they show what a great advantage was enjoyed by their seniors: a man of seventy-four lived through thirty years of peace before the first world war came and has a conception of what man can do when he is not tormented by crisis.

Ignazio Silone must be considered as one of the most attractive of the contributors, full of warmth and generous nobility. But he tells us here only what he has told us so often before, that he was once inside the Communist Party and is now outside it. He writes of people in his case: "For our part, the vital resource which saves us from the extreme situation of nihilism can be easily identified; the same emotional charge which impelled us to our initial choice has not been exhausted by disillusionment." But he does not prove it. He had only fourteen years of peace before the first world war to nourish his nerves, and they have been unequal to the shock of his experiences.

Sartre shows his disability in another way. His contribution comes nearer than any other to the more technical kind of philosophical writing, and even in these brief extracts from his work the command and clarity of his style are apparent.

But his picture of a man as a free creator who builds his own existence depends on the assumption that man can be held to be in the world by his own choice because he could decide to leave it by suicide; and surely this is an assumption born of experience limited to decades of unusual violence and fear of violence. The law is a museum of philosophical concepts which men not primarily interested in philosophy have found in practice to be valid; and the law of coercion holds that if a man is compelled to perform an illegal act under the threat of death he cannot be found guilty of that act. This implies the view that the power to choose self-extinction is not among normal human attributes. It is bracing to realise the impossibility of imagining any scientific experiment or philosophical argument which would prove that the mass of human beings are or are not capable of committing suicide.

Shakespeare was right. There is sometimes nothing to do but say, "But come," and change the subject.

[1] Martin Farquhar Tupper's series of didactic moralisings, first published in 1837, became a huge best-seller in Britain and the United States.

[2] Jacob Bronowski (18 January 1908 – 22 August 1974) was a British mathematician and biologist of Polish-Jewish origin. He is best remembered as the presenter and writer of the 1973 BBC television documentary series, *The Ascent of Man*.

[3] A British weekly Catholic magazine

[4] Followers of Thomas Aquinas

THE SCIENTIFIC OUTLOOK
BERTRAND RUSSELL

THE DAILY TELEGRAPH, Sept. 29, 1931

An unbroken mood of felicity seems to have visited Mr. Bertrand Russell while he wrote *The Scientific Outlook*. It is an extraordinarily gay and inspiring work, full of the good sense that comes from intellectual vitality. If a boy or girl of sixteen can be found who does not like this, they should be removed from school and sent somewhere else; he or she is not getting the right sort of education. For certainly they ought to be amused by Mr. Bertrand Russell's account of Galileo; and might note, if they are tempted to view too crudely the hostility Christianity has at times displayed towards knowledge without sufficient regard for the underlying forces, that the real opponents who stirred up the Church against him were the followers of the pagan Aristotle. Certainly, moreover, they ought to be exalted by Mr. Russell's exposition of how "science in its ultimate ideal consists of a set of propositions arranged in a hierarchy, the lowest level of the hierarchy being concerned with particular facts, and the highest with some general law, governing everything in the universe."

Galileo, as Mr. Russell relates, threw a ten-pound shot and a one-pound shot from the Leaning Tower of Pisa, so that they should arrive on the ground at the same time, to the confusion of the professors who were at that moment emerging from their class-rooms surrounded by the pupils to whom they had demonstrated, according to Aristotelian physics, that objects of different weights would take different times to fall a given distance. Meanwhile, Kepler had proved that planets go round the sun in ellipses, not in the neater circles that Aristotle had preferred. These discoveries led to laws of the lowest generality referring to crude facts, and only a certain number of them. They were put together by Newton, who made it the basis of a law of higher generality, the law of gravitation. And this again was put by Einstein with a law not of physics but of geometry, one that lets most of us be safe when we encounter it in the theorem of Pythagoras, which deals with the squares of the sides of right-angled triangles, and made the basis of the theory of relativity. There is magnificence in the way that the broom of science sweeps up the dust of the earth, flourishes a moment, then is seen above us, sweeping away the darkness from the stars and planets that we may see their orderliness; and then flourishes again for an instant, and sets to uncovering the obscurity that hangs round time and space, the abstract foundations of all other order. Here is matter for young ambition; but not for cocksureness, since there is a chapter handsomely admitting the limitations of the scientific method, which are due to the imperfections of the human mind as an instrument. On the other hand, there is a powerful chapter urging that, however imperfect the instrument may be, one must go on using it, since otherwise we get ourselves saddled with a lot of unprofitable nonsense.

It is a night scene. Mr. Russell leans forth from his casement and sees what Tennyson called "the larger hope" wandering about the garden of the public mind, to which it has been admitted by Sir Arthur Eddington, plucking flowers and singing to itself in the moonlight. His clear, cold criticism descends on the poor thing like water from an inverted jug. Not since Mr. H. W. B. Joseph reviewed "The Nature of the Physical World" in *The Hibbert Journal* has this school been so. He prefers the religious apologists of the eighteenth century, who welcomed the discovery of natural laws as a proof of the existence of a Law-giver, to the religious apologists of today who regard the failure of any of their calculations as proof that a divine element has somehow got into the sum. They seem, he says, "to be of opinion that a world created by a Deity must be irrational, on the ground, apparently, that they themselves have been made in God's image." He deplores as an example the attempts made to use the Principle of Indeterminacy as a proof that physical determinism has not unrestricted sway over the universe, that there is room in it for free will. This Principle does indeed admit that we are not in a position to lay down any law for the movement for the atom, which seems to stagger about without rhyme or reason. A great or at least persistent spiritual teacher, writing in one of last Sunday's newspapers, has described the atom in this respect as behaving like the soul; but it would be at least as accurate to say that it behaves as if it were drunk. And perhaps this also is not an unhelpful conception. The present crisis becomes quite intelligible in its unintelligibility, if we consider it as a pink rat seen by a universe of collectively intoxicated atoms. But this is the most that can legitimately be done with the dance of the atoms in the way of metaphysical speculation, for as Mr. Russell points out, the use to which the Principle of Indeterminacy has been put is due to the double sense of the word "determined." "In one sense a quantity is determined when it is measured; in the other sense an event is determined when it is caused. The Principle of Indeterminacy has to do with measurement, not with causation." The velocity and position of a particle are undetermined because there is now no reliable method known of measuring them; they are not undetermined in the sense of being uncaused. Mr. Russell's advice to the theologians is to leave this argument just where they found it and go home with their hands in their pockets whistling, as at any moment somebody may find out the laws regulating the behaviour of individual atoms. "It is very rash," he points out, "to erect a theological superstructure upon a piece of ignorance that may be only momentary."

But *The Scientific Outlook* makes no cheap pretence that the universe is a box of tricks which any B.Sc. can turn inside out. On the contrary, it passes on to a lively description of what a hell the world would become if there were only science to shape it; and in an eloquent last chapter Mr. Russell declares that though "knowledge is good and ignorance is evil—to this principle the lover of the world can admit no exception," the ultimate usefulness of science depends on the system of values it upholds. "When it takes out of life the moments to which life owes its value, science will not deserve its admiration, however cleverly and however elaborately it may lead men along the road to despair." Edison, Rockefeller, and Lenin, are given the opportunity for domination. "These were men devoid of culture, contemptuous of the past, self-confident, and ruthless. Traditional wisdom had no place in their thoughts and feelings; mechanism and organization were what interested them." They have sought power and not love, although "the satisfactions of the lover, using that word in its broadest sense, exceed the satisfactions of the tyrant, and deserve a higher place among the ends of life."

But, as Mr. Russell says, "the sphere of values lies outside science, except in so far as science consists in the pursuit of knowledge"; and he suggests that if one crosses the road to the sister establishment, art, one will be handed out one's neat little values. As to that one may be doubtful. Is art not very much in the same position as science? Is it not a pursuit of knowledge? Both art and science are alike in that they analyse man's experience; and the fundamental difference between them lies surely in the kind of experience they choose. Science deals with controllable material, which can be observed and measured, and which does not tell lies. Art deals with uncontrollable material, which can be only partially observed and can be measured hardly at all, and which does tell lies; with material, in fact, that is predominantly human. It is however at no disadvantage compared with science regarding the possibility of gaining information about this material, since it has the weapon of the imagination, by which it can put into play in fantasy the psychic mechanism which other people put into play in reality, and record the subjective effect. If science has need for values, it must be true that art also has a need for them.

THE WEIGHT-LIFTER

A review of DOSTOEVSKY: HIS LIFE AND WORK *by Ronald Hingley,*
THE SUNDAY TELEGRAPH, *Aug. 27, 1978*

The Soviet Union, faced with Ronald Hingley's opinions on the Russian people, its literature, its history, its language, and its character, must understand what Lear felt when Cordelia explained that yes, she loved him, but love must be honest even if it meant a knock-out blow between the eyes. In his latest volume, *Dostoevsky: His Life and Work,* as in his 15 earlier works, Dr. Hingley declares himself a Russian-lover who cannot abide what he calls Russian-fanciers.

To understand the situation clearly, turn to his penultimate work, *The Russian Mind.* There he quotes from a revered lady of Oxford, famous for her researches into early Greek religions, who wrote during the First World War (when there was indeed every excuse for Russian-fancying) a pamphlet on "Russian and the Russian Verb," admitting an infatuation with a peculiarity of Russian grammar, the perfective and unperfective aspects of the verb (the first relates what the action did, the second how it felt when it was done, or would feel if it were done).

This she declared to be "a clue to the reading of the Russian soul"; and she went on to confide: "I want to use those aspects. I long to be able to use them, I need them, they feed me spiritually."

At this point, Dr. Hingley happens to mention that the Russian word for "gush" is *umilenye*; and so utterly gooey are those four syllables that one almost thinks him no gentleman for bringing up the matter. But one is glad he committed this breach of chivalry, since it illumines the difficulties he must have found in writing on Dostoevsky.

Piles of *umilenye* accumulated round Dostoevsky, all sorts of things about him fed people spiritually but cannot really have done them any good.

Yet his book on Dostoevsky is deeply respectful. *Umilenye* or not, he says, this was one of the strongest of men who ever did creative work, although Dostoevsky carried a handicap heavier than any we know Shakespeare to have borne. He had an appalling life. When he was 15, his amiable mother died, he had a serious illness, and six months later his father, who was a doctor, lost his sight and had to give up his practice, and break up his home. He left Dostoevsky and a younger brother in lodgings in St. Petersburg, where they were prepared for entrance into the (to them highly uncongenial) Army's Chief Engineering Academy, and he deposited his other five children with relatives in distant Moscow. His family never saw the doctor again. Two years later it was reported to them that he had met with a mysterious death at his country house.

In 1849, when Dostoevsky was 28, he was arrested in St Petersburg for his membership of a group of educated young men who met to discuss such matters as serf emancipation, legal reform, socialism, and revolution. On December 22, on a bitter cold morning, he was the victim of a boorish trick that was played every now and then by the Romanovs. Twenty-one innocents like himself were told that they had been condemned to death and the shooting-squad got ready. The men were tied by threes to posts and clad in shrouds with trailing sleeves and hoods, their hands bound behind their backs by their sleeves and their faces muffled by their hoods. But it was a joke.

Two days later, Dostoevsky had begun his 2,000-mile journey to five years' imprisonment in a filthy Siberian prison, followed by five years' service as a private soldier, still in Siberia: all this time without privacy, all this time fretted by worsening epilepsy.

A writer is not so dependent on his physique as an actor or a musician, or even a painter, but the machine has to be functioning. What is extraordinary about Dostoevsky is that in his case the machine was of deplorable design and he was perpetually ailing. Moreover, he had built-in neurotic tendencies which imposed on him conduct likely to set up all known diseases of stress. He was an untalented gambler, and until he married a second wife who liked shopping and beat him (not too much, but just enough) he could not see a tedious and teasing woman without taking her into his idiot arms. One of the most admirable points in Dr. Hingley's book is his enjoyment of, and respect for, what he calls the impressive reservoirs of mental and physical toughness on which this neurotic, hypersensitive, habitually overreacting, never-relaxing man could draw throughout his life. Many a normal, healthy, un-neurotic person has collapsed under a hundredth part of the burden that Dostoevsky heaped upon himself.

To illustrate the point, Dr. Hingley tells the story of how, when Dostoevsky was saying goodbye to his brother before starting on the journey to Siberia and prison, it was Dostoevsky, though only a few hours had passed since the mock execution, who was the serene comforter. But such moments may be the work of angels and are not infrequent in the history of behaviour. What is more remarkable is the literary vitality which carries this frail and shattered man through his vast and ambitious books.

We must wonder at the skill with which this book manages to be on one level a superb thriller and on another a discussion of the Christian attitude towards moral responsibility. And let us consider the sensitivity towards human relationships.

In *The Brothers Karamazov,* Ivan Karamazov, a hearty, indeed a tough individual, who has really quite a good brain and has therefore been dabbling in matters which usually concern intellectuals alone, has been thinking of the moral future of man, and it has inspired him to write the kind of prose poem which Turgenev sometimes wrote, but longer. He would like to discuss it with his younger brother, Alyosha, whom he loves and respects, but who is alienated from him to a certain extent since he became a novice in a monastery where there is a monk with an exalted reputation for sanctity.

Ivan will not be denied the gratification of his brotherly love, which leads him rightly to suppose that Alyosha can help him through this spiritual crisis. So he takes him out to a familiar restaurant and orders him cherry jam because he liked it as a child and still likes it; and there follows a beautiful piece of work. It is shown how the shyness of siblings may be as petrifying as the embarrassment of strangers and the discussion of such blameless matters as a religious poem can seem as shameful as sexual disclosures; and how the tender discussion of trivial matters can act like magic on the temporary sickness of a relationship.

As to the content of Ivan's religious poem, it grips the mind of every person who reads it for the first time, and wise men of his time wrote volumes of criticism concerning it. But it is prophetic and therefore Dostoevsky erred when he made it so specific. Isaiah and Jeremiah have kept their position through the ages by a certain preference for strictly general denunciation. But Dostoevsky was of the opinion that the Roman Catholic Church (backed, he allows it to be understood elsewhere, by the Freemasons) was going to enter into a curious compact with the human race. Man was going to surrender his free will to the Grand Inquisitor and his company and become their slaves in return for the benefits of government planned not on Christian principles but by the light of reason. Material comfort would then kill the human soul. There could hardly have been a more erroneous prognostication.

To begin with, the deal is impossible. It cannot be doubted that the kind of people who enjoy enslaving others do not enjoy supplying them with material comforts. The Romanov dynasty had already gone to some trouble to give Dostoevsky a demonstration of this by taking away his political liberty but providing him, not with caviar and champagne, but a mock execution. But they could not have kept the promise of material comfort had they wished to do so, for the reason that nowhere has human reason shone so brightly that it has enabled rulers to read the small print and solve all problems of government. The truth is that when Dostoevsky supposed himself to be uttering truths which he had received not from a divine source but from some eternal infinite Horse's Mouth, he was never at his best.

But Dostoevsky's sense hugely outweighs his nonsense. His demonstration of how Ivan's slapdash thinking and coarse feeling inspired his valet to commit murder is a real, penetrating, and novel description of how an ingenious mind can, only half-consciously, but still half-consciously, dedicate itself to evil. And *The Devils* put Dostoevsky on a level with Balzac in seeing intellectual vandalism as the great modern crime. Also he imparts to many of his characters the unique value which is the reason why they should not be vandalised; and it was an indication of his own unique value that he had maintained the strength to do it.

A Master of Humbug

A review of Charles Dickens: A Life *by Norman and Jeanne MacKenzie,*
The Sunday Telegraph, *1979*

Mr. and Mrs. Norman MacKenzie have certainly been coura-geous in writing *Charles Dickens: A Life*, for the great man's life was deplorable. Supposing he had been born in post-Freudian days, one can imagine a psychoanalyst leaping from his chair beside the couch, tearing up his notes, turning his face towards heaven and saying: "Up with this patient I will not put. Back to the drawing board!" To which, after an embarrassed silence, an angelic voice would respond: "Yes, we see what you mean. But, you know, the man is a genius." If the psychoanalyst had guts, he would not accept this. "But it won't do. What's the good of creation if people are like this?"

Charles Dickens was indeed an awful man, and the terrible thing is that he is so awful as to make us laugh when we ought to be weep-ing. When arranging to leave his wife, he wrote to a friend: "Nature has put an unsurmountable [sic] barrier between us, which never in this world can be thrown down."

This is one of the most dreadful sentences ever written, but it is so ridiculously untrue that even Mrs. Dickens might have been startled into bitter laughter. She was 21 when she married him, and in the following 21 years she had had 10 children and five miscarriages.

The MacKenzies know all this and use their admirable narrative gift to good effect. The extraordinary story of how Dickens managed to use mesmerism as a lachrymose way of tricking his wife is very well handled. But it certainly seems at one point that they have allowed the old deceiver to humbug them.

They seem to accept his stories about being a "very small and not particularly taken care of" boy, shamefully neglected by his wantonly improvident parents, especially as regards his education. Surely this is all nonsense.

To begin with, his parents were up against the unfortunate fact that the human species increases at a rate which is usually higher than the rate at which its resources increase; and, like most of the other and uncensured people in this book, they were continually downed by their own fertility. Mr. Dickens was one of the huge covey of minor civil servants to be found in the twin towns of Chatham and Rochester, which were so picturesque that Turner seems the only realistic painter, but are visibly not Golconda.

If his parents did neglect his education, then most parents of this age should be sent to prison. His mother taught him to read before he went to dame school, though she had four other children, and when he was eight he was sent to a highly reputable school kept by a college graduate son of a respected Nonconformist minister. Meanwhile, his father bought the boy a number of cheap reprints of the classics and had him reading *Don Quixote* and *The Vicar of Wakefield* by the time he was 10.

This is not the behaviour of parents who lavished their all on keeping up appearances, and here a small boy may well have misinterpreted the signs of a gallant attempt to retain their self-respect in the face of scandal surely much graver than the MacKenzies would allow. Mrs. Dickens's father, who held a senior Civil Service post, was charged, when little Charles was 10 years old, with the embezzlement of £5,689. Finding's keeping[1] under half-a-crown, but it is not wise to embezzle a sum about 16 times one's annual salary. This event must have been as shameful in the Dickens family as a heavy bank robbery would be today.

The Dickenses had that situation to deal with; and they were also making an heroic effort on behalf of their eldest child, Fanny, who was two years older than Charles. She sang and played the piano and the violin. In 1823, she won a scholarship at the newly founded Royal Academy of Music. Mysteriously, the MacKenzies do not seem to realise that this achievement reflects the greatest credit on Fanny and her parents.

The Royal Academy of Music had its own glory from the very beginning. Its principal, Dr. William Crotch, had begun his career by playing "God Save the King" on a small organ at the age of two, and had thereafter risen, on a steep graph, to greater achievements and had become a very scholarly Professor of Music at Oxford. Most of the pupils were children of professional musicians and had been trained from infancy, and the teacher who supervised Fanny's piano lessons was Ignaz Moscheles, whom the MacKenzies describe as "a pupil of Beethoven," but who was much more than that; he was one of the most famous music teachers in Europe.

Somebody competent in Chatham must have taught Fanny and taught her well, and when Charles was withdrawn from school it may have been for the good reason that his parents were taking sensible steps to put one of their children in the way of earning her living for the rest of her days.

But how the humbug in Charles takes over at this point!

I could not bear to think of myself—beyond the reach of all such honour-able emulation and success. The tears ran down my face…I prayed, when I went to bed that night, to be lifted out of the humiliation and neglect in which I was. I had never suffered so much before.

It is disagreeable that he should have written those words when he was a grown man, and glutted with success, for they are the product of childish envy that should have passed. It was inspired by a prize-giving at the Royal Academy, when his sister Fanny, aged 15, received the silver medal for piano-playing. It must have been a glorious occasion, held in the drawing-room of what had been the town house of the Earls of Caernarvon, with all the male pupils wearing their uniforms, which for some mysterious reason were naval in character, and were finished off by caps which had RAM in gold letters on the band, and a real-life princess giving away the prizes.

Who would not have been jealous of Fanny at that hour? But his emotion had the intensity of unreason and should have vanished at the age of reason. The fledgling musician had power to charm, but writers-to-be have little power to delight audiences. Charles should have realised that as he grew older, had he had any handsomeness of nature.

But his nature was indubitably unhandsome: quite nasty when he talked of young ladies whose fragility of appearance led him to suppose that they might die young. Something in his tone suggested that he would like to have eaten them for his supper, served with slices of lemon and thin brown bread and butter. Of Miss Christine Weller he exclaimed: "Spiritual young creature that she is, and destined to an early death." It is a pleasure to record that Miss Weller married a man called Thompson, lived to a great age, and gave birth to a daughter, who, as Lady Butler, became a firm and authoritative painter of military subjects.

He was nasty, too, when his marriage finally collapsed and he wrote to his housekeeper at his London house, giving her instructions to convert his drawing-room into a bedroom and to close up the door leading to his wife's bedroom with a set of bookshelves. In his mind he was evidently transfusing the situation as between him and his wife: his were the 10 children and the five miscarriages. One sees him standing shuddering in his new celibate refuge, clutching around him his dressing-gown, anticipating that at any moment he would hear the sound of falling bricks and see appearing on the level of the tottering bookshelves, perhaps between two volumes of Boswell's *Life of Johnson* or some such classic, the large face of Catherine Dickens.

He must have been mad; and mad, too, to have driven himself to death for the pleasure of playing before a multitude of sillies the blood-and-thunder murder of Bill Sikes, which is good ham but no more than ham. But the angel would have the last word in his debate over Dickens's soul with the psychoanalyst.

The angel might point out that when there was a General Election and it had coverage, as he thought they called it on television, all the people would look familiar, just because they were all in Charles Dickens's books, written over a century before. A Mr. Callaghan would have Charles Dickens's signature all over him, and a Dr. Owen would look like a character in the unwritten part of *Edwin Drood*. The angel would admit that something had gone wrong. Dickens was not a nice man. But he was also not a man that could possibly be rejected.

[1] An old proverb, sometimes expressed as "Finders keepers, losers weepers."

BRAVE NEW WORLD

by Aldous Huxley

[From typewritten manuscript, Feb. 5, 1932]

Those who are easily shocked had better leave Mr. Aldous Huxley's new fantasy, *Brave New World*, on one side; noting, as they pass, that since this is a free country they are not compelled to read it, this is all they need do about it. Those who are not easily shocked can settle down to enjoy what is not only the most accomplished novel Mr. Huxley has yet written, but also the most serious religious work written for some years. His tendency in his other novels has been to select subject matter which might fairly be described as a fuss about nothing. Even though the characters in *Point Counterpoint* were carefully docketed as interesting individuals, they were, in relation to the depicted imbroglio, as lacking in allure as sexually-maladjusted cockroaches. But the argument in *Brave New World* is of major importance. One could sanely ask for nothing more than it gives.

One would say that the book was about a Utopia, if it were not that a line of dreamers have given that originally non-committal term a sense of imagined perfection; for it describes the world as Mr. Huxley sees it may become if certain modern tendencies became dominant, and its character is rather that of deduced abomination. If one has a complaint to make against him it is that he does not explain to the reader in a preface or footnotes how much solid justification he has for his horrid visions.

It would add to the reader's interest if he knew that when Mr. Huxley depicts the human race as abandoning its viviparous habits and propagating by means of germ cells surgically removed from the body and fertilised in laboratories, so that the embryo develops in a bottle and is decanted instead of born, he is writing of a possibility that biologists are seeing not more remotely than, let us say, Leonardo da Vinci saw the aeroplane. And it would add to the reader's sympathetic horror if he realised that the society which Mr. Huxley represents as being founded on this basis is actually the kind of society that various living people, notably in America and Russia, and in connection with the Bolshevist and Behaviourist movements, have expressed a desire to establish; and that this is true even of the least pleasing details.

There is, for instance, one incident which immensely enhances the impressiveness of the book if one knows its counterpart in reality. In this new world there are various grades of human beings to do various work, running from Alphas who hold all the positions of power and do all the intellectual work, to the Epsilons who do all the drudgery and are too stupid to read or write. These are all bred for the purpose from selected germ-cells, exposed to various treatments during their bottled stages, and then educated by various devices depending on the theory of the "conditioned reflex," which holds that any animal or human being can be taught to dislike an object, even if it is inherently pleasing to them, if it is always presented to them in association with an object that is inherently unpleasing to them. Mr. Huxley gives an example of one of these devices.

The Delta babies, who are being bred to do menial work that demands a certain amount of intelligence, are put down at one end of a nursery, at the other end of which are set out bowls of roses and open picture books. They were allowed to crawl to them and lay hands on both the roses and the books; but as soon as they settled down to their play the nurses press a lever which lets loose a babel of sirens and alarm bells. The babies go off into screaming fits. Then, to rub in the lesson, the strip of floor where they are lying is electrified, and the babies shriek and writhe with mild electric shock. This device serves two purposes. Since the Deltas have to perform fairly intricate work, they cannot be bred below a certain fairly high level of intelligence, above that which would make it possible for them to read or write; but since the community cannot afford to have them waste their time on what must necessarily be a fourth-rate mental life, it seeks to make books hateful to them. And it has to discourage any native love of flowers, because they are not machine-made; and the appetite of citizens must be directed away from the natural to machine-made goods, so that the nightmare of over-production may be laid for ever.

Now, the interesting thing about this experiment is that it is in technique exactly the same as those constantly conducted by Dr. John B. Watson, the founder of Behaviourism, a philosophy which has probably made more adherents in the last twenty years than Christian Science did in the last twenty years of the nineteenth century, and finds them in a more influential grade. "I hope some time to try out the experiment of having a table top electrically wired in such a way that if a child reaches for a glass or a delicate vase, it will be punished, whereas if it reached for its toys or other things it is allowed to play with, it can get them without being electrically shocked." He believes in "building in the negative reactions demanded by society"; and the society he belongs to is one that would certainly, if it could, have demanded such reactions as Mr. Huxley's new world demanded from the Deltas. Was it not that society in which, just before the crash, a conference of automobile manufacturers expressed that intention of "stimulating the two-car sense"?

There is, indeed, nothing at all impossible in Mr. Huxley's vision of a world where the infants are conditioned by such experiments, and by the dormitory loud speakers that whisper moral education into their sleeping ears (his pages on hypnopaedia, or sleep-teaching, are among the most amusing in the book) into a lack of all characteristics save those which tend to uphold the stability of the state. Much of it is actual in America. There is this salesmanship, which enjoins them to make a division between that which is valued and that which is preserved; they are taught to acquire an infinity of gimcrack objects, display them, throw them away. They are taught to dissipate their force on silly crowd pleasures. The talkies have become the feelies, but have not changed their fatuous essence. The chemists have found that drug they have been looking for, which intoxicates without deleterious effect on the nervous system. Leisure hours therefore become a blandly drunken petting-party; for promiscuity is a social duty since it discourages, far more than Puritanism, the growth of that disintegrating factor, love.

The religious instinct has been transferred by skilful conditioning to a deity known as Our Ford, whose beautiful and inspired sayings such as "History is bunk" are reverently handed down. Age has disappeared, youth is artificially prolonged till sixty, when there comes death which is not feared. We are privileged to visit now a co-educational establishment under the headship of Miss Keate, a free-martin (for details refer to the first chapter of the book) and see five busloads of her pupils "singing or in a silent embracement," rolling home from Slough Crematorium for a stage in the death conditioning which begins at eighteen months. Every tot spends two mornings a week in a Hospital for the Dying. All the best toys are kept there, and they get chocolate creams on death days. They learn to take dying as a matter of course. Emotional and intellectual life is entirely flattened out, so that the State which supplies the material needs of the citizens shall run with a triumphant smoothness, as it is intended in Bolshevist Russia. If the individual is drowned, at least he is drowned in a bath of communal happiness.

Into this world comes a Savage: a white child who has been born, through certain odd circumstances, in an American Indian reservation which has been kept untouched for psychological research reasons. His mind is governed by the harsh conceptions of Indian religion. He believes in the vileness of man that can be made acceptable to the gods only by fasting and scourging, and again scourging; so that blood must be drawn from the back if the gods are to let rain fall on the pueblo and the corn grow, and the delights of love must be fenced away by restriction upon restriction, and cancelled afterwards by shuddering loathing of them and contempt for the object who afforded them.

Towards those who begot or conceived one (so obscenely, compared with the decent technique of bottling and decanting), one is fixed in a torturing relationship of loving concern which it is almost impossible to destroy. Far from blood and hatred and anguished passion being eliminated from life, they are ritually preserved; and nothing is done to veil the threat that, at the end of all this agony, there is nothing but a door painfully opening into emptiness. To this harsh existence there are no palliatives save the joy to be found in hunting and dancing, in the craftsmanship of the potter and the weaver: unserviceable aesthetic joys. It happens that the Savage has found in the Indian Reservation an old volume containing the works of Shakespeare, an author forbidden in the new world on account of the reprehensibly private nature of the emotions he chiefly describes. They supply him with an almost complete language to express these blood-stained primitive beliefs; since the poet, also, for all that the literature teachers have done to disguise it (as one may read in a very entertaining essay by Mr. Lytton Strachey), held beliefs not very different.

The Savage is, therefore, aware of his own world. It is not merely strangeness that makes him detest the new world and use the more denunciatory passages from Shakespeare to express what he thinks about its arrangements. "Goats and monkeys," he cries, like Othello, and, at their sexual freedoms, "But to the girdle do the gods inherit, beneath is all the fiend's." He finds contentment everywhere, but no nobility. Relief from the fear of death is no gain. As he sees his mother die in the Hospital for the Dying ("something between a first class hotel and a feely palace, if you take my meaning," says the nurse), doped with the new drug, canned music, and perfumes, while Epsilon dwarf identical twins munch chocolate éclairs round her bed as part of their death-conditioning treatment, he realises that to know the terror of death is better than to be drugged out of that knowledge. As he says when he talks to Mustapha Mond, one of the ten World Controllers, a cynic who reads Shakespeare, too, behind locked doors, things are too easy. One pays no price and one gets nothing valuable. He quotes Othello again: "If after every tempest come such calms, may the winds blow till they have wakened death." And though Mustapha answers that no experience can be as valuable to us as the happy absence of experience, it is plain that he regards his own answer as an inferior expedient.

It is only at the end of the book that one sees precisely what literary task Mr. Aldous Huxley has set himself. He has rewritten in terms of our age the chapter called "The Grand Inquisitor" in *The Brothers Karamazov*. In these days Dostoevsky is out of fashion, partly because he writes with heat and passion of the sort that Mr. T. S. Eliot's sham classicism has taught us to despise, and partly because the simple and elephant-sized neuroses of Tolstoy are easier for the inattentive eye to follow than the subtle spiritual ferments of Dostoevsky. But "The Grand Inquisitor" is a symbolic statement that every generation ought to read afresh. In it Christ revisits earth, works a miracle in the streets of Seville, and is immediately by order of the Cardinal thrown into the prisons of the Inquisition. He visits the captive in the middle of the night and tells him that he has recognised him as the Christ, but means to burn him at the stake, because he insists on the freedom of man, and man cannot be happy unless he is a slave, "'For now !' [he is speaking of the Inquisition, of course] 'for the first time it has become possible to think of the happiness of men. Man was created a rebel; and how can rebels be happy?'" The words are almost the same as Mr. Huxley's World Controller's.

But instead of the Inquisition, instead of the orthodoxy that in the nineteenth century crushed spiritual endeavour, Mr. Huxley is attacking the new spirit, so ramified and pervading that it lacks a proper name, which tries to induce man to divert in continual insignificant movements relating to the material framework of life all his force, and to abandon the practice of speculating about his existence and his destiny. Equally a denunciation of capitalism and communism, so far as they discourage man from thinking freely, it is a declaration that art is a progressive revelation of the universe to man, and that those that interfere with it leave men to die miserably in the night of ignorance. The book is many other things as well. One could cover many columns with discussion of its implications. It is, indeed, almost

certainly one of the half dozen most important books that have been
published since the war.

SOVIET CAMPS: WHO'S GUILTY?

A review of THE GULAG ARCHIPELAGO II *by Alexander Solzhenitsyn,*
THE SUNDAY TELEGRAPH, *June 25, 1978*

The third volume of *The Gulag Archipelago*, Alexander Solzhenit-syn's great work on that darling child of Stalin's heart, the system of Corrective Labour Camps which he scattered over the Soviet Union, is written by a great, awkward, obstinate, coura-geous, unaccommodating, immensely gifted Russian, who hates his country's misdoings and loves his country. That is his trouble in writ-ing this book. The enterprise is no easier than composing a novel in praise of one's wife but making no secret that she is a murderess of great technical gifts and unlovable energy. But it is only fair to warn English and American readers that they will have their own trouble over this great work.

The existence of these camps, and of their predecessors as designed by Lenin and Trotsky, has been known to large numbers of the English-speaking population for many years. There is a remarkable woman in our midst named Iulia de Beausobre, a woman of obvious probity and intellectual distinction, in later years known as the beloved and loving wife of the great historian Sir Lewis Namier; as long ago as 1938 she published a classic account of the sufferings she endured in a prison and a prison camp, to which she had been consigned for her first husband's unproven and in any case unimportant differences of opinion with the Soviet Government. She was only one witness among many whose evidence of maltreatment closely agreed.

A large number of politicians and journalists would have none of this. They said these witnesses were liars, prejudiced against the dawn of a new society. They were unmoved by other witnesses who gave another sort of evidence. These, such was the venom of their prejudice, went so far as to suggest that their state was even worse. They lay still, and stopped breathing, and even were buried.

This overwhelming testimony was contradicted largely (and falsely) in the Western mind by visits from British and American lovers of Lenin and Stalin, of whom the most bizarre was perhaps that severely handicapped Vice-President of the United States, Mr. Henry Wallace.

During his tour of the Soviet Union, Mr. Wallace was taken to one of the most notorious camps, where large numbers of people had formed this disingenuous idea that they were dead. Mr. Wallace seems to have taken the camp for something like the equivalent of British Leyland[1]; and he was strangely moved when he was presented by the authorities with a tomato from a camp greenhouse. It made him feel that everything was all right. Such an unsubstantial basis for optimism has not been presented since Pippa passed[2].

This is a grisly thought, though Russians cannot turn up their noses at Mr. Wallace. Had he been born in Russia he would have probably been a venerated *staretz* such as we have read of too often in Russian novels.

But it is surely obligatory to spare a shudder for all the competent smarties, the Press and civil servant sub-culture of Washington and the great sky-scrapers of the media, who led Mr. Wallace like a lamb to the place of other men's slaughter. It is dreadful to think that if they had not procured this repulsive act of buffoonery there were hosts of their own kind that would have done it in their place. Let us remember that 25 years ago a large part of the Western European and American population of intellectuals were, with disgusting single-mindedness, pimping for Stalin.

This was partly because our economically unsettled world demanded the establishment of some kind of support for our intellectuals which would work like the patronage afforded to Grub Street by the moneyed aristocracy in the 18th century. There were material advantages to be gained by friendly toleration of the KGB, delightful connections and a sense of adventure. Some sincerity there may have been, but not much; for they found it as impossible to believe in the sincerity of their opponents as if they had never heard of that attribute.

They accepted Stalin and the tomato; and 25 years ago Solzhenitsyn would have had great difficulty in having this volume published in Great Britain and America. And indeed his path even now will not be clear of difficulties. Dark rumours are already spreading that he is not *chic*. And of course he is not: people out of camps rarely emerge in that state of temporal grace. But there are other forms of beatitude.

Therefore, Solzhenitsyn's work should be read with diligence. One will see how completely indefensible the institution of the camps was from the first and how, after the death of Stalin and Beria, the correspondence and policy of their successors openly admitted the truth of the charges which had long been disregarded by the Soviet apologists in the West.

The mischief of this tampering with the truth is revealed very clearly in this volume. Those who wished the truth to be told were not moved (as was often said) by the desire to inflame Western populations with a desire to make war on the Soviet Union. Any candid revelation of the horrors of the concentration camps must make it plain that these problems could not be solved by any form of foreign intervention. No external power could destroy the system or replace it with one that would be better; it is too vast, its existing structure would be impossible for any but Russians to sweep away. The problems of closing the Nazi concentration camps were incomparably easier, though they were great enough.

What alone would reform the Soviet concentration camps is criticism from the rest of the world, based on accurate facts and, above all, not tinged by prejudice which refuses to admit that regarding the foundation of such institutions the Soviet Union was under special temptations. As *The Gulag Archipelago* shows, the Tsarist State had left behind it a long tradition of resort to punishment by exile, which was cruel in its separation of the individual from his environment, but was so sluttish in its administration and so mitigated by humanitarianism that it was not efficiently cruel. But in post-revolutionary conditions it was bound to become an inferno.

The growth of the general population and the acute political paranoia of the new order which increased the number of convicted dissenters to authority; the number of nations within the Soviet Union who have their own languages and cultures and therefore were in poor communication with a central Government which felt more and more need to communicate with them; the decay of humanitarianism inevitable in any country where the forms of government increase fear instead of diminishing it, which is the prime psychological task of government: all these are the handicaps of the Soviet Union which no other Power could remedy by any form of aggression. We can do our best by pointing out what seems to us offensive in the Soviet system to a nation which is, as *The Gulag Archipelago* proves, intensely sensitive to opinion and extremely anxious to improve its credit.

All these and many more facts relevant to the situation are presented by Solzhenitsyn, as well as story after story that admits us into the hearts and minds of a great people tortured by their history. But what gives the book its value is the sound it gives out; the harsh roar given out by a wise and experienced animal as a warning that the herd is in danger. Solzhenitsyn makes that necessary noise very well.

---

[1] British Leyland was a vehicle manufacturing company partly nationalised in 1975 and renamed in 1986 as the Rover Group.

[2] Robert Browning's poem "Pippa Passes" is about an innocent, young girl passing through a city steeped in corruption. The most quoted passage is:

The lark's on the wing;
The snail's on the thorn;
God's in his Heaven –
All's right with the world!

THE AGE OF CONSENT
BY EVELYN FANE

THE NEW STATESMAN, June 10, 1922

In an evening newspaper lately, Dean Inge wrote an article on modern fiction, and (after pausing to recommend the works of Mr. Archibald Marshall and a "charming little book called *A Vagrant Tune*") pronounced fiction to be in the mass vulgar and indecent. It is extremely difficult to debate whether he is right or wrong, for tastes differ so widely concerning what constitutes vulgarity and indecency. We can concur readily enough in a vague definition of the qualities. Both find their delight in the exhibition of the human organism in such a way as to bring ridicule upon it and its functions, but vulgarity does it laughingly and openly and without losing its moral sense, while indecency has a secret smile and a hope that enjoyment will end in sin. But we differ enormously in our recognition of these qualities. The writer must make up his mind that in these matters there is no pleasing everybody.

I myself have been accused of the graver offence when I hardly expected it. In an essay on Henry James, I happened, when discussing his indifference to abstract thought, to use the phrase, "He never felt an idea with the sensitive finger-tips of affection." I was startled to receive a press-cutting from an American newspaper, in which a reviewer protested against the use of "this sensual metaphor in connection with a writer of the known purity of Mr. James." None of us can provide that our innocent inventions may not be seized on by such persons as this and used as bases for the horrid dreams of their own engendering. Was not *Man and Superman* seized in the American mails on the petition of the deliciously named Dr. Mabel McCoy? It is for this reason that, on the whole, artists make a point of abstaining, so far as possible, from discussions on the decency or indecency of works of art, and of discouraging them where possible. It is not that they like indecency, but that they know that if any persecution is started in the name of decency the standard that is adopted is as likely as not to be one invented by one of these mephitic minds.

But now that this question of indecent fiction has been raised by Dean Inge, who is intelligent enough, though not so intelligent as it is fashionable to allege, it is as well to examine certain current assumptions in order that next time the question comes up it need not be in quite such an idiotic form. Embedded in Dean Inge's article, which seems to have been written on a day when he was not burning with a hard, gem-like flame (it contains such great thoughts as "Broad comedy, such as we find in Dickens, is admissible in fiction, though it is not a very high form of art"), are the opinions that "a corrupt following of Continental models, French and Russian, has introduced both vulgarity and indecency into the most modern English fiction," and that our novelists write this stuff in order "to cater to the corrupt taste of the moment."

Now, these assumptions crop up every few years or so, usually in a sermon by one of the Higher Clergy, who seem a class terribly addicted to the pleasures of the libel. The form is different every time (there was a Canon once who thought of a particularly good line: "I would rather send my daughter into a house infected with diphtheria than let her read *Ann Veronica*"), but the spirit is identical. There is always the same allegation that most novelists spend their time writing obscene

books, getting rid of their handicap of island purity by accepting polluted inspiration from certain always un-named Continental models,
and that they do this with the intention of making money.

One wonders how this legend begins. Does theological training
destroy the power of enjoying fiction as (according to Darwin) scientific
work destroys the power of enjoying poetry? By the time one becomes
a Dean or a Canon, is the water-gruel of Mr. Archibald Marshall all
that one can digest, so that one shrinks from ordinary adult fiction like
a sickly dyspeptic from a beefsteak? Or is there a lunatic who spends
his life and wealth writing, printing, and publishing improper books
and introducing them (by innumerable minions stationed in the post
and railway offices whose duty it is to tamper with parcels to and from
Mudie's and the *Times* Book Club) into the homes of the clergy? There
must be some such explanation, for those of us who range freely among
books, who have the advantage of seeing practically the whole yield
of fiction gathered together on shelves for us to choose from, can find
no such stacked masses of lasciviousness as the clergy suggest.

Let us try and trace these people, who form "a corrupt following
of Continental models, French and Russian." Reflection tells us that
there are none. There never was a time when literature was less affected by the influence of France, and though Turgenev and Tolstoy and
Dostoevsky and Tchekhov have great power over the writers of today,
this hardly acts in the direction of vulgarity or indecency. Can it be that
the Higher Clergy was talking through its hat? Can it not! The truth is
that probably not two percent of the year's published novels could be
called vulgar or indecent by any person of normal standards. It must
be remembered that to write a book which holds up to ridicule the
human organism and its functions is a difficult achievement. A writer
may start deliberately to be silent concerning the mind and the soul and
write of nothing but the corruptible flesh. But as the French proverb
has it, the most beautiful girl can only give what she has got; the facts
of human physiology are few and obvious, and to save his story from
thinness any artist has to keep hailing back the mind and the soul. And
these are instruments which preserve man from ridiculousness, since
even in their failure they arouse pity, so great is the difference between

man and the bright pattern by which he plans himself.

When one goes on and examines the other assumption, that the writers of indecent novels are consciously prostituting their pens for gain, the argument becomes profoundly disquieting. The only objectionable novel I can find among this season's yield was plainly not so written, for its author is full of that contempt for earthly consequences which (like much else of the mental quality that inspires her story) is strong at the time though probably quite amenable to psycho-therapeutic treatment. This book (enticingly named *The Age of Consent*) tells the story of a girl of seventeen whose parents, after exploiting her as an artist's model, try to induce her to go away to the country with a vicious rich man. The girl is rescued by a young artist, but to save him from being prosecuted for abduction she returns to her parents and goes by appointment to the rich man's studio. But he, out of revenge for his first disappointment, sends in his stead a criminal lunatic who assaults the girl. There are pleasing descriptions of him in the detention cell, "clutching a piece of soft white underclothing. 'I tore it off her,' he muttered, 'into shreds; what a sight she looked when I had done with her…You should have seen her when she knew she could not get away.'" Ten years later, when the girl has married her rescuer, who has become a peer, the lunatic is released as cured. The peeress's friends freely inform her of this, chatting over the tea-cups; and when he writes and asks if he may call, she says he may, and is a little afraid that her "letter sounded cold and formal." He comes to tea several times, and it is all very pleasant; but on his last visit he goes into the butler's pantry and strips the clothes off a housemaid who resembles the peeress. The butler goes and tells the peeress. ("'Is he still in the pantry?' she asked. 'I think so, your ladyship, but he does not seem quite himself.' The butler still looked dazed and confused. 'I think he said that your ladyship would understand, but I may have heard wrong.' 'I will be down in a minute,' she said.") When she went down, the lunatic dropped the housemaid and murdered the peeress by breaking her ribs, and after covering the corpse with a tablecloth went and threw himself into a pond. Subsequently, the family solicitor found a locket round the housemaid's neck which indicated that she and the peeress were illegitimate half-sisters. So there, in a manner of speaking, we all are.

Now, what Dean Inge and all those who indulge in this periodical ramp about vulgar and indecent fiction ought to note about this volume is that it has no relationship whatever to contemporary literature. There is no sign that the author has ever read anything. The book is the expression of her individual mental obsession which is the characteristic of the really objectionable book. Mr. Joyce, again, is a lone soul working on his own, and his plumber-like view of the universe is, again, no novelty to students of abnormal psychology. It must clearly be recognized by Dean Inge and his kind that this really objectionable department of fiction is a phenomenon by itself, and that to blame the literature of the day for its quality is as absurd as it would be to lecture the inhabitants of Middlesex because the inmates of Hanwell and Colney Hatch[1] have delusions. And they should recognize also that when one analyses a really indecent work, one invariably finds that it is a fantastic expression by which the author relieves himself of the trouble stored up by some early suppression; that he is misrepresenting life because in his youth he was not allowed to understand it. He feels that he is doing something right in writing ugly books about squalid interpretations of life, because he was brought up in an atmosphere where people read fatuous books about smug interpretations of life and wished that Mr. Hardy would not write novels like *Jude the Obscure,* and were capable of launching frivolous indictments against the finest of the arts.

[1] Insane asylums, both in Middlesex

THE MYSTERIOUS MAUD

A review of MAUD GONNE *by Samuel Levenson,*
THE SUNDAY TELEGRAPH, *Aug. 28, 1977*

T he women loved by Yeats drift through his pages like wraiths of mountain mist, but in reality they were big, big girls, and the biggest of them all is the subject of Samuel Levenson's volume Maud Gonne, the biography of an impassioned Home Rule agitator. By general consent, she was a splendid sight, with red gold hair and huge hazel eyes and a superb figure, richly formed to give back the bullying corset of the day as good as it gave.

In her photographs she seems isolated by her amplitude, and so she was. Yeats's love was poured out on her for many years, and she did not notice, but rushed past his courtship like the last bus on the way to the terminus; while Yeats had the aspect of someone waiting at a bus-stop in a drizzle as the pitiless vehicle went by, golden and glowing, through the dampness of the night.

Indeed she was a human bus. She invaded the territory of the Irish Home Rule movement, dedicating to it her glorious presence, her thrilling voice, her instinctive command over the technique of turning a street-fight into an historic occasion. This she was able to do only because she was as insensitive as a bus, for while her proceedings enraged the British authorities, many Home Rulers liked them hardly better, since she was pure English. There appears to be no ground for supposing her to have had a drop of Irish blood in her veins. But on she went, crashing past the lights to give aid to Cathleen Ni Houlihan.

But Maud Gonne also possessed a quality odd in so large a person. She was invisible at will. Throughout at least a dozen years she played a conspicuous part in Irish social and political circles, while she was also conducting a passionate love affair in France as the mistress of a Right-wing politician named Millevoye, to whom she bore two children.

True, this trait is almost irritating; her power of covering her tracks would have been so much more useful to the Irish cause had it been bestowed on Parnell and Mrs. O'Shea. But it nevertheless speaks of a certain command over circumstances for a large woman to divest herself of a dramatic private life so completely that all the Dublin gossips were left with was an erroneous impression that she was the beautiful woman in whose arms, as people say, President Félix Faure had breathed his last.

Readers will certainly enjoy this volume, though it is a pity that not only Maud Gonne, but her biographer, seem far departed from the normal pattern. Proof-readers seem to shun Mr. Levenson; it is unlikely that when Maud Gonne appeared before Yeats in flowing robes in his poor Bloomsbury lodging she was wearing a gold toque round her throat. A toque is a small bazaar-opening hat; but a torque is a necklace such as was worn by early Celts. Certainly a torque would be Maud's choice. Time, also, is no friend to Mr. Levenson. It is unlikely that in the early 1880s MacGregor Mathers, a Dublin magician, was courting the daughter of Bergson; the great French philosopher was then in his early twenties, and the lady has been identified elsewhere as his sister.

But a worse influence still on the volume is the seepage through the text of those Left-wing views, far gone to decay through the action of moth and rust, which we have now to expect from studies of European subjects coming to us from American sources. There is a most odd passage about Maud Gonne's birth. Her father and representatives of her mother's family signed a marriage settlement on December 18,

1865, and on the next day, December 19, the wedding took place. Mr. Levenson asserts that on the third day, December 20, the bride gave birth to Maud, and garnishes this unlikely news with a comment so bizarre that one cannot help suspecting that he must be somehow involved with the social sciences:

"If true, it says a good deal about Maud's father, and about the society in which marriage settlements could continue to be heavily bargained when the birth of progeny was imminent."

To enjoy fully the perversity of this comment it must be noted that the bride belonged to a fabulously wealthy and highly respected family of import-export traders named Cook, and that the marriage took place in the parish church close by their stately home; and that the bridegroom was the son of a prosperous wine-importer, who was making a career in the Army and was about to set up house in Aldershot. All parties were not the sort to bring to the ceremony the element of suspense hoped for by Mr. Levenson as signs of capitalist sin.

Maud Gonne's world was strange enough without such fantasies. It had its virtues. It was sincerely anxious to do better than previous generations had ever done. But it is disconcerting to find that the same community was waterlogged with the practice of magic on an infantile level. Its members, even those of genius and talent, were all up to their eyes in astrology and table-turning and home-grown myths and rituals that worked out like school plays.

This weakness was to some extent pardonable, as it afforded light relief from the perpetual idealism of the Dubliners of the time. Those of us who have joined societies for the furtherance of noble causes would often have felt it a relief if, like Maud Gonne, we had found one with a chairman who believed he had been a tiger in a previous incarnation, and felt warmly toward any female member whom he suspected might have been his striped and four-footed mother.

And there are some enchanting glimpses of Madame Blavatsky, founder of the Theosophical Society, to whom only the pernickety will deny the gift of style. Superb is her vision of a Shadow Cabinet of angels, using the Himalayas as their Whitehall till it was time for them to take over the government of the world, as many civil servants have ached to take over from our faulty Parliament; and it was of real appositeness to the political conditions that have established themselves in the hundred years or so that have succeeded since her prophecies.

There was some genius in Mme. Blavatsky, and endless fun. In these pages there is a charming vignette of the old lady, in her Dublin days, despising her followers when they took the flickering of the gas chandelier over her séance table as proof that the dead had risen from their tombs. "Flapdoodles," she called them. The term, uttered by a lady who looked like a bloodhound born in the purple, becomes Miltonic. That Maud Gonne preserved these anecdotes proves that she must have had a sense of humour, and indeed that was not her only good quality.

She conducted a campaign for giving free meals to Irish schoolchildren, which was a much more sensible way of spending the time than the agitations that preoccupied many of her political associates. She seems to have been kind and loving to her family and friends, with a hard-wearing, homespun affection.

As to her failings, though Yeats was right in the bitter lines he wrote of how she raised anger in the streets, it must be remembered that till recently none of us have had any but a partial view of street-fighting. During all previous riots, those who were reluctant to have issues settled by the broken bottle stayed at home; and those others, to whom assault was a favoured sport, went out into the streets and whirled their arms and legs and saw little, since such activities impair vision. The reality of street-fighting could not be realised till television was developed to its present stage. Now everyone knows the truth, and all who disregard their knowledge are offenders against civilisation. But it was not so in Maud Gonne's day, and she can be counted guilty only of the lesser offence of proving, beautifully but a shade too expensively, that a bull in a china shop need not be male.

BUSY LITTLE
WORKER BEES

A review of BOLSHEVIK FEMINIST: THE LIFE OF ALEKSANDRA KOLLONTAI,
by Barbara Evans Clements; and THE YAWNING HEIGHTS,
by Alexander Zinoviev, translated by Gordon Clough
THE SUNDAY TELEGRAPH, *Apr. 29, 197?*

The fate of the Tsarist Empire was largely due to the excessive addiction of the educated classes to two unprofitable activities. One was belly-aching: the conversion to a grievance of each and every circumstance (even when quite neutral) in the belly-acher's life, and the use of it as proof of the superiority of the belly-acher, and the inferiority of his or her family.

In a graphic picture of this sport as practised by a brilliant performer, turn to *Bolshevik Feminist: the Life of Aleksandra Kollontai*, by Barbara Evans Clements, an Assistant Professor of History at the University of Akron, who is fortunate among her kind for her possession of a lucid and pleasing style.

To grasp the arbitrary nature of belly-aching, it must be realised that Kollontai's parents were admirable people who, though they were near-aristocrats, were liberals, never afraid of acting up to their principles even when this involved them in danger. But, their daughter felt and proclaimed, they tortured their little one. Her mother made her put her clothes on a chair when she went to bed and be polite to the servants. When Aleksandra desired to marry a young engineer, her parents rightly divined that she was not really in love with him but was attracted to him only to annoy them, and with relentless savagery they postponed her marriage and left her withering on a bough, till 1893, in which year she was 21.

She then produced a child whom she handed to the servants in order that she might concentrate on reading Marx and writing fiction, but her husband trespassed on her time. He wanted her to spend some of it with him, the brute. When she explained that she had other and more cultured ideas, what did he do? Why, the low cad said he would engage more servants so that she could spend all her time writing.

Oh, woe, woe. But she then had an article (on child-rearing) accepted and in her elation she waited till her husband was called to South Russia to do some work, then parked her child on her parents and took a train to Zurich in order to study Marx freely, sending a letter to her husband which gave him the first intimation she was leaving him. Dr. Clements calls this "a cruel and somewhat cowardly" action, but what is really remarkable about it is its speed. Not only had she done all this, she had spent hours in reading Marx, uninvited, to her husband, and there had also been rustlings in the emotional shrubbery which suggest a love affair, actual or contemplated. But she had been married only four and a half years.

Then, of course subsidised by her father, she abandoned herself to the other addiction which was bringing Tsarist Russia to its knees: constant and impassioned attendance at Left-wing committee meetings and conferences. Unfortunately, all gatherings convened for the betterment of the human lot show a tendency to gas themselves, and not with laughing-gas either. The conflict between the will to benevolence and the will to power produces cracked enthusiasms, cracked resentments, and an inability to count, and a general sense of insecurity is engendered; and lo, there descends among the faithful the demon of intrigue.

This second sport was not at all to Kollontai's taste. She was, except when a victim to the fashion for belly-aching, a good-hearted girl with many virtues; and one of them was her comradely feeling for other women.

When she set about giving this kindly feeling a practical form, she learned to her astonishment that the Russian Communists were bitterly hostile to feminism. What they felt about it she learned when she arrived at party headquarters to hold a meeting of her officially and hypocritically sponsored Women's Bureau, got to the room which had been assigned to her, and found it locked, with a notice on the door: "The meeting *for women only* has been called off. Tomorrow a meeting for *men* only..."

The excuse of the male Communists was that, as the purpose of the party was to precipitate a revolution, giving women the vote and feeding underfed women and children was a diversion of funds and energy, and anyway it might benefit bourgeois women. This was a pretext. As for funds, they could always have robbed some more banks, and as the parliamentary system would have to be destroyed it could not have mattered who had votes. The truth was quite simply that the boys wanted to go on clobbering the girls, according to custom.

Gradually, Kollontai perceived that truth, and also began to experience the power of committees to nurture vicious performances in the way of intrigue. Lenin, especially, was never above kneeing this simpleton, who was always almost comically on the level. As her enemies grew more distasteful, the less she was able to cope with them. By the time Lenin died and Stalin succeeded him, she was into her fifties and worn out by disillusionment.

The rest of her life was touching. She made compromise dignified. She was sent abroad as a diplomat, that she might no longer try to reform the party and would be forced to defend the policies she detested. But she made the best of it. She had loved Finland and the Finns since childhood. It fell to her to negotiate the peace treaty between the Soviet Union and Finland in the Second World War. She did her best to mitigate the Russian vengeance: but she could not do much, and it was not long before she suffered a wrecking stroke and went slowly down to death, which must have seemed a happy escape from backbiting and treachery.

Against all expectation, *Bolshevik Feminist* is more interesting than *The Yawning Heights* by the dissident philosopher, Alexander Zinoviev. It could be a novel, if it were a novel. But it is a sort of symposium collecting the opinions of contemporary Russians on the many defects and some merits of the Soviet form of government. But Plato himself could not have captured our attention if Socrates had presented his material in a form as unattractive as a juggernaut lorry full of close-pressed, cold porridge.

Its 829 pages provide few new reflections. We must have already known that while all failure is humiliating, it must be specially humiliating, should one feel compelled to make lavatory jokes, not to be able to make good ones. This is a terrible book quite unadapted to the human power of absorption. But the publisher tells us that the author wrote it in six months, and it would be extraordinary if anybody wrote a good book of 300,000 words in six months.

Haste has been Mr Zinoviev's ruin, and we grieve over the occasional revelations of his real quality, which may be admirable. There are vignettes of people who are professionally clever, and are cleverer than most people, and yet not as clever as most people—which reminds us of our own Malcolm Bradbury's studies of English and American universities.

Better still, there are some touching passages about the ecological tragedies of man's political environment. One deals with the way ideologies can establish themselves within the minds of a people without being subjected to any real criticism; another is a touching elegy on the death of the Russian intelligentsia, and what it was in its glory. The first is on page 288 and the other on page 735. One reports these locations in the spirit of a faithful sherpa carrying the stores up to the right camp sites on Mount Everest.

THE MAN WHO TOLD TOO MUCH

A review of RN: THE MEMOIRS OF RICHARD NIXON,
THE SUNDAY TELEGRAPH, June 11, 1978

Richard Nixon's *Memoirs* have been issued in a format that would do credit to any undertaker. It is a shiny coffin of a book, and it should be sold with some small Meccano-ish form of hearse, fitted with an attachment which plays a recording of the Dead March in "Saul." This is entirely misleading, for the great value of the work, extracts from which appeared in *The Sunday Telegraph*, is its demonstration of resilience. It gives the readers hope that should they fall from the top of the Eiffel Tower a short stay in hospital will set matters right.

This bouncing quality might be the result of stupidity or impudence, but it has nothing to do with either. It is caused by a peculiarity of Mr. Nixon's mind, which would present a danger were it widely possessed.

Richard Nixon has a shrewd eye for facts, but his mind is so unsophisticated and so narrowly educated that he has almost no mental context. He calls up facts from the vasty deep and they do come to him, but once ashore they have nowhere to go. There is no homeland where they can settle down and establish relationships with the facts which got there earlier or come later. But each fact as it turns up has to give its name and number, and the result makes a much more concrete and useful work than most produced by the politicians of his time; while at the same time it is obviously at odds with reality, it could not have anything but a sad ending; a very sad ending: death in life.

It is really very lively for the memoirs of an eminent person. To quote a Chinese proverb (used by Joseph Conrad when reviewing a book of short stories written by a colonial governor, up till then his close friend), "It is rarely given to the Emperor that he should excel as a flute-player."

But Mr. Nixon is quite good. True, he has his faults. If it be ungentle-manly to kiss and tell, it is still further from gentlemanliness to pray and tell; and he should have got a Dickensian friend to strike out all passages which bring to mind the name of Chadband. But Mr. Nixon still manages to tell us much that we did not know before, because he has the colours of reality on his palette.

If readers should take the trouble to collect a pile of annuals cov-ering the past few years and check with these memoirs on the globe-trotting of Mr. Nixon and Dr. Kissinger, they will find they get a new sense of what those trips were like, and what they gained. But on the other hand, a cloud of uneasiness will gather. Mr. Nixon reports things it was not wise to report, and he involves himself in them, but not as a conspirator in a dirty business. Rather, he seems a simpleton who does not understand that people do not wish to learn how silly their species can be, particularly when it is demonstrated by individuals whom they have elected to represent them on the supposition they are specially wise.

Few rituals are so absurd as the international confrontations be-tween what are called the great Powers, quite inaccurately, for the lesson of recent history is that the large Powers can no longer be the great Powers. The first stage of such meetings is stuff for the zoologist: the most powerful male on the host side and the most powerful one on the other side strut up and down in front of each other, uttering hostile cries, varying in vehemence according to the conditions. As Mr. Nixon shows, Mr. Khruschev greatly enjoyed this stage of the proceedings, putting so much into his hail-gorilla-well-met manner that it cannot be wondered that his fellow-countrymen ultimately wearied of him.

There follow the negotiations, in which more use is made of the human invention of language. Then there is a period of relaxation: the parties chiefly involved put their feet up in solitude and return refreshed to the final negotiations, which were, on some of the occasions described by Mr. Nixon, sensible submissions to reality.

It is the period of relaxation which Mr. Nixon describes in one instance with such ominous imprudence. During a visit to China, he and Chou En-lai took their leisure in a beautiful guest house on "The Island of the Two Towers Reflecting the Moon" which floats on a lake near Hangchow. They twaddled together, as tired people do.

Chou En-lai read some poems by Chairman Mao, and was apparently not at his expository best. For one is left with the impression that one poem began with something like, "Plum blossom is a lovesome thing, God wot," and went on to claim, "Not Marx! in gardens! when the eve is cool?" This seems improbable. But Chou En-lai went on to discuss another poem with more lamentable results: "This poem was written after a military victory over the enemy. In the whole poem there is not one word about the enemy; it was very difficult to write this poem."

To this Mr. Nixon twaddled back: "Of course, it is very useful to think in philosophic terms," and followed up that reflection by six sentences containing no philosophic terms whatsoever, and indeed conveying no meaning whether considered singly or together.

He had obviously no suspicion that the conversation, which he no doubt accurately reported, confirmed the awful suspicion which walks closer at our heels every day we live, that perhaps the chief reason for the unhappiness of the human race is that it is not very clever. Useless to plead that the two men were tired; useless to plead that that particular confrontation was not unfruitful. Up it comes, the anxious question, "Are these the men who are deciding my national fate?" And what is quite certain is that Mr. Nixon had not the slightest idea that he then, or ever, provoked that question.

This blindness was a dangerous defect to take to Washington, which is itself not a safe place. The United States devised its Constitution and made Washington its political centre when it was a small nation, and now it is immense. Because its political centre is detached from most of its social and economic centres, it is isolated in spirit, unsupervised, unrestrained, and often seems to enjoy the obsolete freedoms of a Gold Rush city.

As the whole country necessarily turns its eyes on the seat of its Government, a vast number of journalists settle there, and vie with each other in the search for sensational news, while the national Press of America is dwindling, so there is far more specific political news than discussion of political principles. There are many opportunities for sensationalism, since Washington is so difficult to organise, in its boiling and bubbling state, that it is burdened with many obsolete procedures which give occasion for charges of corruption. The inhabitants overact like the cast of a melodrama on a night when all the critics have been invited.

In such a community, Mr. Nixon was quite oddly helpless. Many people are more or less unconscious of the effects they produce, but his blindness was abnormal; and he often gave Washington what he had good reason to know it would not take.

That city has often accepted politicians with wives as crazy as coots, but it has to be the right sort of coot. Nevertheless, Mr. Nixon made John Mitchell his Attorney General, though he had been his partner in a law firm for seven years and knew him to be a slow and awkward man, with a wife who, poor dying lady, was as crazy as the wrong sort of coot, and certain to be an embarrassment to Nixon's Republican party and an enduring joy to his Democratic enemies.

It was also all to the bad that Mr. Nixon had allowed his aides to choose a White House staff which were bizarre beyond belief. They resembled Bret Harte goldminers, O. Henry's Broadway types, and, indeed, characters out of science fiction. Sitting among these grotesques, which makes anything Downing Street has suffered from of late years seem normality itself, Mr. Nixon offended all standards, not only in Washington, but anywhere else in the world where one could possibly be.

He confesses, with some embarrassment, but not enough, that when a civil servant purloined some letters from papers from the Pentagon, he felt it right and proper to order his staff to burgle the office of this man's psychiatrist and steal his papers.

It is obvious that by then Mr. Nixon had fallen a victim to his special defect. He was not a political monster, inspired by malice against persons, classes, industries. He was simply not aware of that prejudiced organ, the other man's eye. The incident in itself showed blindness to the diminishing repute of psychiatry in the last 20 years.

Thereafter, his days were packed with the dubious. In the odd way that happens only in the wrong political circles, huge amounts of money began to flow along unsanctified channels. He treated his two aides, Haldeman and Ehrlichman, with a disloyalty that shows he had forgotten the ties of humanity; he drowned them as if they were kittens.

Then there is a catastrophe in which more than Mr. Nixon is involved. One of his staff, Howard Hunt, oddly enough a writer of some merit, received a huge draft of those mysterious dollars and sent his wife to deposit them in Chicago. The plane crashed, she was killed, Hunt fell into deep melancholy, seeing himself as her murderer. The story then takes off, it becomes much more than one man's memoirs, it becomes a myth, a graph of misfortune, a diagram showing how the cancer cells of tragedy develop.

It is all most unfortunate, and not only for Mr. Nixon. The quality of Mr. Nixon is not exalted and neither is the quality of the campaign America has waged against him. The value of the Presidency must be depreciated for some time to come; and it is always a pity when lightning strikes a country's landmarks.

THE GATHERING STORM
THE SECOND WORLD WAR, VOLUME 1

by Winston S. Churchill,
THE SUNDAY TELEGRAPH, June 28, 1970

M r. Churchill's account of the events leading up to the Second World War and its first awful year, which subjected us all to ordeal by stagnancy, is a puzzling book. It is clear as crystal about everything except the man who wrote it. That clarity, so far as it goes, is beyond price, and we must thank Heaven that when it decided to complicate earthly affairs, it provided a chronicler with the vitality to cope with that complication. This is not to say that Mr. Churchill's style always pleases. He is not nearly so good at the style which Sir Walter Scott called "the big bow-wow" as he thinks he is. His rhetorical passages seem, like the first English automobiles, to be preceded by a man carrying a red flag. But in his less flamboyant moods he is a master.

He is without match in his generation for his exquisitely feline portraits of his enemies. The spiritual essence of the late Earl Baldwin was described when he was but an infant in Truthful James's poem about the Heathen Chinese; but to draw him as he was in his temporal circumstances has baffled his contemporaries. He was apparently both honest and a humbug, and nobody can figure out whether his honesty was a ruse adopted by his humbuggery, or whether he was so honest that he never saw when anybody, even himself, was being a humbug. In a few urbane sentences Mr. Churchill suggests what the political game was like when he does a like job for Neville Chamberlain. But in the latter case he pulls his punches. It has evidently struck him that if a man is told that a number of persons living in a house are cripples, he may leap to the conclusion that that house is a Home for Cripples. Winston Churchill is the leader of the Tory Party, and he is not going to make it lose face altogether. So, though he gives Baldwin away completely and frankly reveals Neville Chamberlain's incompetence at certain periods, he preserves certain reticences.

An example occurs in connection with the visit to London of Henlein, the Nazi leader of the Sudeten Germans in Czechoslovakia, in 1937. He fails to say that Henlein came to London as the guest of an influential Tory family, who were most energetic in inviting guests to meet and be deluded by this organiser of revolt in a friendly country. Mr. Churchill may have been moved by his feeling, which is entirely correct, that the Tory family was inane rather than mischievous. But all the same it is a slight falsification of history.

But apart from this partisan tenderness Mr. Churchill has served history well. He has an unsurpassed gift for exegesis. This book can be recommended to everybody who wants to keep by them a handy record of what happened between the end of the First World War and the beginning of the second. It lays out the tangled events of those twenty years so that not the least instructed mind can fail to see that when Dollfuss ran in hopeless hope to save his life from side to side of the pit in which he was snared the bells of English and American churches should have tolled for their own dead. His literary gift enables him to describe a certain manifestation so odd, so out of the run of reasonable life, that it would defy a less accomplished pen: the intrusion of the barbarians cherished and chosen as emissaries of the Fascist powers, into the familiar world of ordinary manners and morals.

The particular barbarian who astonished England was Ribbentrop. He knew how to dress according to the customs of Western man; but apparently all other customs except those relating to coats and pants and hats were beyond his comprehension. It was as if a robot had been appointed Ambassador to the Court of St. James. One had thought his most astonishing performance had been at Buckingham Palace where he gave the Nazi salute so grotesquely that the King smiled kindly and the whole Court tittered. But Mr. Churchill relates with considerable art an even more extraordinary scene which took place when Ribbentrop and his wife attended a lunch-party with Neville Chamberlain during which news came of Hitler's invasion of Austria. The description is tartly amusing; but it also conveys the chill which it is reasonable to feel when one finds that a person with whom one is transacting an important matter accepts none of one's conventions and is therefore an incalculable quantity. Having shown how these ponderables and imponderables made a war, Mr. Churchill then takes on the task of teaching the general reader something of tactics and strategy, and in his chapter on Norway makes a job of it as prettily intricate as a well-composed fugue.

But the whole book is puzzling. When it tells the story of the world's progress to its second total war, it has to tell the story of Mr. Churchill's own life; and that propounds a mystery. He is the most able statesman of his time, and he foresaw the most dangerous threat to his time. Yet his political life has been a matter of shunting from one to the other of the older political parties, and finding security in neither, and finally being thrown out into the desert by the Tories for the best part of a decade during which he held no office at all, though these were the years preceding the war, when his special naval and military knowledge should have marked him as indispensable to the Government. He was made Prime Minister only when Great Britain was in the extremest peril of death, and once he had averted that peril he was ejected from office.

It is a tragedy; for humanity produces so little genius that it needs to avail itself of all there is, and this is a warm and attractive genius whom one would not willingly slight. But it cannot simply be put down as crass ingratitude, for that theory demands that too many people in too many different circumstances should decide to practice the same far from universal vice to a pitch which challenges their sense of self-preservation.

This volume indicates that some of Mr. Churchill's difficulties with his colleagues may have been due to his phenomenal egotism. At the end of the chapter celebrating his return to the Admiralty at the beginning of the "phoney war," he strongly recommends a practice which, he says, "greatly extended my daily capacity for work. I always went to bed at least for one hour as early as possible in the afternoon and exploited to the full my happy gift of falling almost immediately into a deep sleep...I regretted having to send myself to bed like a child every afternoon, but I was rewarded by being able to work through the night until two or even later—sometimes much later—in the morning, and begin the day between eight and nine o'clock." This may be so; but it is ominous that Mr. Churchill shows no consciousness of the fury which this practice inspired in all his subordinates, who were obliged to keep the office hours of the services to which they belonged and were therefore not able to go to bed in the afternoon, but who nevertheless found themselves summoned to listen to the Prime Minister's bright ideas till the small hours.

To counterbalance such inconveniences there are, of course, firework displays of wit and clowning and wisdom. But the inconveniences are there, together with a defect not uncommon in great men. There must be only the small-sized round the throne. Professor Lindemann, now Lord Cherwell, is the only man of eminence mentioned in these pages as a familiar friend, and there is not such mention as might have been expected of the many public men who never ceased to protest against his exclusion from office. But other statesmen have had far more discouraging attributes without detriment to their careers. Mr. Gladstone had a habit of delivering to any company in which he found himself short lectures on such subjects as the history of violin making, but suffered no harm.

It helps us to uncover the mystery, perhaps, if we consider the identity of the colleagues of Winston Churchill who worked hardest for his exclusion from politics. One was Earl Baldwin, the other was Neville Chamberlain. The one threw Mr. Churchill out of power in

1931, the other refused to let him back till the enemy was at the gates. Both, though Tories, were arrant demagogues. It was Earl Baldwin whose apology for not having warned England that Germany was outstripping her in air power has become a classic of political cynicism. "Supposing," he told the House of Commons, "I had gone to the country and said that Germany was rearming, and that we must rearm, does anybody think that this pacific democracy would have rallied to that cry at that moment? I cannot think of anything that would have made the loss of the election from my point of view more certain." Lately this utterance has been whitewashed by Tory defenders (among whom Mr. Churchill ranges himself in a half-hearted paragraph) who pretend that he was moved by the fear that if the Socialists got in they would do even less for national defence than he meant to. But as that amounted to hardly anything it is difficult to see how he could have cherished that fear. There is much to show that he cared in the simplest and the grossest way for the favour of the people; and so did Neville Chamberlain, who wanted so much to be popular that he could not believe in England's determination to be rid of him even when teams of postmen were using sacks to carry to 10, Downing Street the telegrams demanding his resignation. If these two men excluded Mr. Churchill from their Cabinets, it must have been because they thought that he was displeasing to the electorate.

In this opinion they were, in an immediate and personal sense, quite wrong. When the electorate sees Mr. Churchill walking down the street or hears him over the radio it likes him very much indeed. It likes his infantile contours, his several optimistic and epicurean chins; the gusto with which he munches his juicier phrases, particularly if they cock a snook at his enemies; his easy and beaming possession of the first requisite of manhood, courage; his rich solemnity, which shows him aware but not afraid of pain and death; his preposterous clothes, which are obviously the cast-offs of a hippopotamus. The very sight of him sends a crowd into sudden, tender, familiar laughter. Yet, as the polls show, the demagogues were right. The crowd is ambivalent towards Mr. Churchill. It loves him, it distrusts him, it fears him. Why? There is a hint at the answer to be found in what might seem a very unlikely quarter, in the second section of Beatrice Webb's autobiography, which has recently been published under the title of *Our Partnership*.

Beatrice Webb was a brilliant member of the wealthy middle class thrown up by the industrial revolution, who came to maturity during the last decade of the nineteenth century and who died during the Second World War. Her book describes how she looked round at the dissolving society of her day, foresaw the rise of a new political party which would determine its programme according to the interests of the enfranchised working class, and decided that that party should adopt the conception of government by administrators dedicated to the service of the collectivist ideal. She was immensely successful in realising her ambition, and the intellectual section of the Labour Party, which supplied the British Government with its Prime Minister and most of the more conspicuous members of its Cabinet, is her child.

Our Partnership is a solemn warning to those who believe that Left Wing political movements must necessarily be an expression of love for the people. Love was not the animating principle of Beatrice Webb. She had a deep affection for her husband, Lord Passfield, but hardly even liked the rest of the world. Her instinctive hostility to the human race always flared up when she met a new and definite personality; and when she met Winston Churchill it erupted like a volcano. The relevant entry in her diary threw up flame and lava. Her impression of him was wholly mistaken. She alleged that there was "no notion of scientific research, philosophy, literature or art" in the man who was to exploit scientific research as no other statesman has ever done before, to write not one book but many which make all serious writers regard him as their comrade, and to qualify as a sound painter in the academic tradition. Almost as comical was her assertion that he was "without capacity for sustained and unexciting labour," for he has always been, in the most sedate periods of peace as in war, a superb administrator. But the temperature of the entry is very interesting indeed, for it shows that he falls into the category of those people of whom she disapproved most vehemently, and we know from other entries in her journal who these people were. She disliked working class socialists quite considerably; there is a quite blistering passage about an International Socialist Congress which "approached raving imbecility."

But what she really hated were Dukes and Duchesses. She shuddered with hatred on every occasion when she was brought into contact with any of the old aristocracy who, on a foundation of landed property, had formed the governing class until the new industrialists like her father had arisen to divide power with them. She found them arrogant, and without the title she would have admitted gave them a right to arrogance, for they were stupid. If she disliked Winston Churchill at sight, it is because she knew that he belonged to this class by birth, and assumed that he was a member of it by nature also. Forty-five years have passed since the first meeting of Winston Churchill and Beatrice Webb, but that suspicion still walks the earth, and is the prime cause of his unpopularity. So far as it survives on the Left it is due to the actual influence of Beatrice Webb, who bequeathed to the intellectual section of the Labour Party a disposition to class hatred far more vicious than is felt in the section which stems from the Trade Union movement. But it is also felt on the Right, because Earl Baldwin and Neville Chamberlain and many of their Tory followers came of the same class as Beatrice Webb, the class which felt abashed and nervous before the class which had had power longer than they had and had therefore learned to fear nobody and swagger and, it might be, push, and tie up all inhibitions in the family kennels.

That is why England has always kept Winston Churchill. Behind him they see the bowers and parks of the great houses which were the nerve centres of the old order; in him they fear the insolence which was the occupational disease of those who lived in the great houses. They suspect that, given his head, he will ride down the common man. It is interesting to read *The Gathering Storm* with an eye on the evidence it offers for and against this charge. There is some support for it in his views on certain international matters. In his estimate of the factors operating at the end of the First World War which caused the Second World War, he names "the complete break-up of the Austro-Hungarian Empire by the treaties of St. Germain and Trianon." He remarks, quite inaccurately, that "there is not one of the peoples or provinces that constituted the Empire of the Hapsburgs to whom gaining their independence has not brought the tortures which ancient poets and theologians have reserved for the damned."

He should know that the treaties of St. Germain and Trianon did nothing to break up the Austro-Hungarian Empire, for the reason that it had already fallen to pieces. The First World War broke out because Vienna was a moral ruin, ostensibly dominated by the two warring courts of a senile Emperor and his neurotic heir, and actually the prey of an irresponsible military caste; and the peoples whose independence was recognised by the Treaties were happier than they had ever been before, until those Treaties were annulled by the Second World War. He is wrong about the Irish Treaty Ports. He makes heavy weather because in 1938 Neville Chamberlain handed back to de Valera the rights Great Britain had enjoyed under the Irish Settlement to use as naval bases three ports in Eire, all of which could have been valuable fuelling bases for destroyers hunting submarines in the Atlantic and protecting convoys. There is no doubt that Mr. Chamberlain was moved to cede them by a wholly imbecile confidence that there would be no Second World War.

Yet, even as a stopped clock tells the right time twice a day, so this foolish man's foolish decision coincided with what the highest wisdom would have seen as the proper course. For had we used the Irish Treaty Ports as naval bases, a number of Irish patriots, with nothing else to do and possessed by a serene confidence that Great Britain was in any case strong enough to be victorious and save them from an Irish invasion, would have sabotaged our enterprises with the utmost courage. This might have subjected us to serious losses and would have raised hostility to us among sentimentalists all over the world. Another issue on which Mr. Churchill raises our doubts is his opposition to Indian independence.

He parted with Earl Baldwin over his policy of Devolution, which surely was another example of a stopped clock telling the right time. Earl Baldwin was the laziest of men and was inspired to his policy by nothing more than a yawning acquiescence in current talk of liberal ideas, but nevertheless it recognised the disequilibrium caused by the whole-hearted resistance of the Indian people to the half-hearted occupation by the British people. In fact, in these instances he ignores the will of the peoples of the defunct Austro-Hungarian Empire, the Irish people, the Indian people, and the British people, and so proves that there are some grounds for the general suspicion of him.

But he has a fine record as a maker of democratic England in his various periods of office. Beatrice Webb took back all she said of him in a footnote which calls him "progressive and able." He was strongly sympathetic to Mrs. Webb in his attitude to social legislation, and often conferred with her. An entry in a later volume shows him staffing the Labour Exchanges he set up with young men whom she had recommended to him. He wanted to abolish poverty; and other inequities too were his enemies, it seemed. There is a note in the Appendix to this volume which consists of extracts from his Admiralty minute book which shows him leaping to the defence of three candidates for naval commissions who, after passing well on their written examinations, had been turned down on social grounds. No Labour Minister would have gone further. Yet again, we are bound to remember when we read his contemptuous references to Mussolini that he was one of the first to hand orchids to the Duce, and very orchidaceous orchids they were.

We find ourselves to the very end of the volume balancing this against that, making the sum come out odd, making it come back even. We sigh in astonishment at the fools who year in, year out, kept out of power the man to whom we British owe our lives. (For we do that. If he had not been with us in the summer of 1940, we would have run up and down and been destroyed.) But that is the story told in the first volume. There is the second volume yet to come. Did the stopped clock tell the right time then too? Did the fools, with the clairvoyance which is sometimes given to compensate for foolishness, foresee Teheran, Yalta, Potsdam, all the terrible matter that will have to be explained in that second volume?

WINSTON'S
PROP AND STAY

A review of CLEMENTINE CHURCHILL *by Mary Soames,*
THE SUNDAY TELEGRAPH, *June 24, 1979*

O
n page 96 of Mary Soames's admirable biography of her mother, *Clementine Churchill*, she tells a story which goes straight to the heart of the matter. In 1913, Mrs. Churchill, as she then was, was staying with Winston Churchill's cousin, the Duke of Marlborough, at Blenheim. She was at some disadvantage. She was without her husband, as he was occupied with the duties which fell on him as First Lord of Admiralty in the Liberal Government under Mr. Asquith; and at many other places this might have been taken as a good reason for his absence, but not at Blenheim.

That tremendous palace was a citadel of Toryism, and Winston had gone into Parliament as a Tory Member (like his father, Lord Randolph), but had crossed the floor of the House to join the Liberal enemy. Clementine Churchill was also handicapped by her youth: she was in her twenties, and, until her marriage five years before, she had been an aristocratic waif.

Her childhood had been frightening. Her mother was the beautiful maverick daughter of an impoverished Scottish earl, and her father behaved like the mysterious stranger in a Gothic novel, though he was by trade the secretary of Lloyd's. Clementine's adolescence was shadowed by the death of a beloved sister, she was not allowed to stay under the protection of a much-loved teacher and go to a university, and when she grew up to be a society beauty she was too poor to buy the right clothes. She was in love with Winston, but they had no money and a growing family and she was deep in debt, and, because of her childhood, she loathed insolvency.

It can easily be realised that she was not in good training to bear up against the railleries of Blenheim, which came at their object like flying sandbags. The Duke enjoyed teasing her about the alcoholic indulgences of Mr. Asquith, and this revolted young Clementine's loyalty to her husband's chief, so she asked him to forgo this pleasure, particularly when the butler and footman were in the room. This made the Duke repeat his little jokes more audibly. Then, in the middle of luncheon, a telegram to Clementine arrived, from Lloyd George, relating to some plan with which the Churchills and he were involved, and she left the table to write a reply.

The Duke of Marlborough, apparently forgetting that he was not only that but also a Prince of the Holy Roman Empire, behaved not at all picturesquely. He achieved, probably without effort, a sentence which was equally offensive whether it was meant seriously or as a joke. "Clemmie," he said. "Would you mind not writing to that horrible little man on Blenheim writing paper?"

What did Clemmie do? Why, the grand girl left the room, went upstairs to her bedroom, rang for a maid to pack her cases, ordered a cab to take her to Woodstock station, swept past the Duke in the hall, and went back to London, where, it is regrettable to say, she got only half-hearted support from Winston.

The terrible thing about this story is the effect it has on the reader. Do we shed tears in sympathy with poor Clemmie? No, we do not. We are too busy exclaiming, "Oh, how I wish I had seen her as she swept down the staircase into the hall, past the Duke, and into the cab!" She must have looked superb, in her own way, which was uncommon.

There was something masculine in her beauty, a look of a young man painted by Giorgione, though she was also a Van Dyck lady, glowing in expectance of some magnificent pleasure, a masque or a dance in a great hall.

But that cannot have been what she wanted. She must have longed for everyone to be as loyal as she was, to be as simply savage as herself towards dukes and princes who did not keep the rules. She must have hoped for government by chivalry. But she got neither that, nor enough rest, nor quite what any woman wanted in a husband.

It would be wonderful to receive, through a long married life, as many love-letters as Winston Churchill sent his wife. But most women would agree that it would be disconcerting to get so many love-letters which were so much alike. And what wife, if she accused her husband of unfaithfulness, would not be infuriated, did she receive such a disclaimer and rebuke as she got from Winston? "And it offends my best nature that you should—against your true instinct—indulge small emotions and wounding doubts." It could have been chiseled on a tombstone, and it is the point of such matrimonial cries of distress as hers, that the tomb is not the place where they are uttered. Victims of jealousy, a grief peculiar to life, should be comforted in loving and living accents.

It has to be admitted: Winston Churchill as a husband chills the blood. How awful, for a woman with five children and never quite enough money, to have to put up with the constant stress and strain of her husband's catastrophic reactions to the apparently simple problems of living at Chartwell! It makes one feel ill to look at the photographs registering the changes he made in that unhappy structure, which must often have wondered what had hit it.

Why, if he felt like that about it, did he not buy another house in the first place? And how lamentable were those attempts at making artificial lakes, where, had they ever been fully constructed, the water would always have had a troubled appearance, since the streams that fed it had had to climb so vigorously uphill. And one's heart breaks for Lady Churchill when her husband proposes that their cattle pro-gramme should be shifted "from beef to milk." As well might he have ordered poor busy Clementine to take an oar in a galley. It is to be noted that this biography shows her to have been accident-prone to a quite remarkable degree. Again and again she broke her poor beautiful bones. It is said to be a protest disease, a complaint against overwork. We can believe it. "From beef to milk," indeed.

These activities cost us all dear. Lady Soames makes two rather perfunctory allusions to an elderly American diplomat named Lewis Einstein, whom she sees as the owner of a large car, in which he "trundled" Lady Churchill about when they were both spending the summer in St. Moritz. He was actually an extremely able servant of his country who had ended his career very creditably as Ambassador in Czechoslovakia between the wars; and he had a retentive memory and a mastery over the spoken word which enabled him to give on demand a bright account of any important international crisis in modern history.

Hearing these two talking together after dinner in St. Moritz was to learn what the world lost because Lady Churchill was over-worked by her destiny. Refreshed by the mountain air and delicious food, she would sit at leisure, and there would stir in her mind some long-standing curiosity about a crisis that had happened before her time but within his, and she would ask questions. "Weren't you *en poste* at Istanbul when there was that terrible massacre of the Armenians, that someone wrote a book about called *The Forty Days of Musa Begh*? How did all that happen?" The old man would always answer well; but on those evenings he answered even better than his custom, because of her questions, that cut deep in to the mind. She could have done much more than she did had she not done as much.

And in her excellence there was variety. She had great wit. "Tell us," someone asked during one of these evenings at St. Moritz, "did you get marvelous caviar from Stalin during the Russian honeymoon?" Humour flashed in her eyes, and she composed a history of the early days of British films in 19 words. "As a matter of fact, Stalin never gave us as much or as good caviar as Alexander Korda[1] did." And while all her hearers laughed, she laughed too, as if pleased at scoring a rare success.

[1] Sir Alexander Korda (September 16, 1893–January 23, 1956) was a Hungarian-born film director and producer, and a leading figure in the British film industry, as producer, director, and founder of London Films. He was the first film director ever to be knighted.

QUEEN ELIZABETH, BY J.E. NEALE

THE DAILY TELEGRAPH, Feb. 4, 1934

O nly the incurably light-minded will wish that Professor Neale's *Queen Elizabeth* was a word less than its three hundred and ninety pages. It is an ample, detailed, and most admirably readable work, the most pleasing amalgam of scholarship and literary brilliance, which avoids the prime error of most biographies of Elizabeth and does not make a mystery where there is none simply because she was a woman. He shows her as a complex of characteristics quite logically assembled by an exceptionally lively germ cell to meet the demands of her environment. She was a Renaissance woman; she answered as did every ardent spirit to the call to learning which rang through Europe in that day; and she had that other Renaissance characteristic, of seeing life as infinitely malleable, as material to be hammered into all sorts of strange shapes, by all sorts of instruments, of which craft and lying were not particularly discredited.

She was a woman born and bred in danger. Professor Neale's early chapters describe how uneasily this poor child of a beheaded mother lay in the lap of her step-sister's displeasure, how the romping companionship of her step-mother, Catherine Parr, and her new husband, the Admiral Seymour, was doubled with the darker stuff of danger, how, Catherine being dead in childbirth, the Admiral Seymour declared himself Elizabeth's suitor and was immediately killed. Fear and its anti-body courage determined her character; the rhythm of their succession ran through her moods till her dying day.

This was perhaps the cause of her love of dress, her wardrobe of three thousand costumes; for it may be remarked that the women most famous for extravagance have been those, like the Empress Josephine, who have lived for long in peril of their bodies. It was certainly the cause of her abundant possession of irony, that laughing sister of affliction who is sent from above to comfort the brave. That salted her whole life. It made her able to convert the lying letters princes must write into comic masterpieces of humbug, and diplomatic conversations into wild "rags."

That last conversion makes one wonder whether, had she not been a queen, she might not have made her mark in another world. She was certainly a genius as a prose-writer. Professor Neale says that she was the victim of a euphuistic habit "which was to grow into a curse, making her studied writings insufferably obscure and involved," but that is only true of the occasions when she had to lie. When she could puff out her chest and write with pride, her phrases sped like arrows to their mark. That her literary talent went further than this, that she might have been a dramatist of the first order, is hinted by the comedy, played not with imagined characters, but with real people out of the Spanish Courtship.

Philip of Spain, widower of her dead step-sister, Mary, kindly proposed to marry Elizabeth, both because he would thereby bring back England to the Papacy as a service to God, and because he had found her exceedingly attractive when he came over to attend gloomily on his bride. Elizabeth had not the slightest intention of marrying him, but she wanted him as an ally, so she played a subtle and maddening game with his Ambassadors. The first, Feria, after committing himself to the opinion that Elizabeth was "a young lass who, although sharp, was without prudence," staggered home with a leg which had been so often pulled that it must have looked like a bell-rope. The later Ambassadors—who came after Philip had in despair married the King of France's daughter, and there was only the political alliance to arrange—might have been supposed to have an easier task. But they too suffered acutely. Feria's successor, Archbishop Quadra, wrote:

"Your Lordship will see what a pretty business it is to have to treat with this woman, who I think must have a hundred thousand devils in her body, notwithstanding that she is forever telling me that she yearns to be a nun and to pass her time in a cell praying."

There is a specifically feminine humour about this occasion, though one must be careful not to assume there was anything else specifically feminine about the occasion. The dilemma in which she found herself regarding marriage is often spoken of as if it existed only because she was a woman; as if it were only because she was a female sovereign that, should she choose a spouse abroad, her country might fall under foreign influence, and, should she choose one at home, civil wars might start among the great families she had slighted or honoured by her choice. Yet that was a danger that constantly arose in the case of kings, that had led among the French to the establishment of the convention that their king must have a wife from a foreign royal house, but a mistress who was born and bred in France. The French Monarchy never fell till Louis XVI disregarded this convention.

The only thing peculiar to Elizabeth's dilemma was that, as Professor Neale points out, each of the horns of this dilemma meant a further horror than itself. It meant that she had to submit to political impotence, while handing over her power to someone who would almost certainly be inferior in intelligence to herself, who would have to deal with the financial problems that drove even her genius nearly demented.

"No national debt; no long-term loans; annual income a quarter of a million, increasing under stress by a further sixty per cent; only with this in mind can the story of the war period be appreciated."

Her advisers were of little help. When she tried to balance her budget, Walsingham sighed, "I would she did build and depend on God." Cecil was sometimes as unhelpful, and Leicester, sent abroad with an army, raised his own and his officers' pay to an extent that wrecked her schemes for financing the campaign. Her suitors, from Philip of Spain and the Archduke Charles down to Arundel and Pickering, were even less promising aids.

Elizabeth's reluctance to marry had therefore, Professor Neale holds, a largely political explanation; and there is not much sense in writing as if Elizabeth's constant willingness to consider marriage-plans, and her invariable custom of baulking at their fulfillment, were signs of a neurotic disposition that was particularly unbalanced on the subject of sex. For every time she chose to announce her willingness to marry, it had the same effect on the courts of Europe as a herring thrown to a flock of gulls, and so long as she did not marry she still had the herring for next time.

As for the coquetry and flattery of her own court, Professor Neale has an interesting paragraph:

"...The internal peace of the country turned on keeping the no-bility, like butterflies, chasing round a candle, spending their wealth on the relatively harmless but prodigal ways of Court life. Courtiers themselves proffered the solution of the problem, for the adulation which they would have given to a king quite naturally became tinged with the admiration, flattery and coquetry which they used towards an attractive young woman. Thus, by a paradox, sex, having created a problem, itself solved it, and the reign was turned into an idyll, a fine but artificial comedy of young men—and old men—in love. Being without precedent, it was a little shocking to the unimaginative—it still is; but it secured service, which it was a monarch's function to do, and charged service with emotion, which it was Elizabeth's desire to do. Her genius rose to the game. Her royal sense, her intellectual temperament, her quick mind and repartee, kept it artificial enough for safety; her humanity saved it from fatuity."

On all the aspects of Elizabeth's life about which biographers become most whimsical and luxuriant in their imaginings, Professor Neale preserves a most pleasing good sense; though he surely goes a little too far when he likens Elizabeth's supervision of the morals of her court to that of Queen Victoria. It is true that Queen Victoria would have been enraged with any of her ladies in waiting who anticipated or secretly indulged in marriage; oddly enough, in the case of the unfortunate and maligned Lady Flora Hastings, she behaved with much more crudity and cruelty than Elizabeth ever showed in a like case. But Queen Victoria did not fly into a violent rage when any sturdy peer of her realm, say Lord Warwick or Lord Ripon, got married, and insist on them keeping their wives down in the country. Without doubt we must allow that in Elizabeth there was burning a fire of the most peculiar flame. But it is Professor Neale's particular virtue that he shows how she kept this fire damped, how her genius usually had the upper hand of her oddities.

He shows special shrewdness in the case of Leicester and Essex, who are known beyond all shadow of a doubt to have been Elizabeth's favourites. But that word can in our tongue be used either to mean an animal who is expected to win a race or to cloak from infant eyes in history books the more picturesque of royal potentialities. We will never know which sense of the word can be fitly applied to Leicester and Essex; and it is possible that Elizabeth herself hardly knew from day to day. It is possible that here we are dealing with a situation that falls under no usual categories. For Elizabeth must have thought masculinity a very odd thing. She was herself a most truly feminine woman, for she was one of the very few women who have been born in a position where they could determine their own lives, and look in their own hearts for feminine standards, and who have the brains to use that opportunity. Masculinity was her opposite. It was bound to be the thing which she could least understand, to which she was most attracted. All her life it presented itself to her in a most lethal guise. Her father had beheaded her mother; she knew that Jane Seymour had pined away after the birth of a Prince and Katherine Howard had given her head to the block; she had seen her step-mother, Catherine

Parr, die in childbirth and had seen her half-sister, Mary, pushed down a slope to craziness and death by her husband, Philip. And after she grew up, her relations with men have been summarized by Mr. Milton Waldman, another admirable biographer, in the concise and startling sentence: "The number of men who tried to assassinate Elizabeth in the decade preceding the Armada exceeded the number of those who wanted to marry her during the previous two."

It was small wonder that she preferred her relationship with men to be one of firm government. But just sometimes she seems to have reflected that this masculinity must play some useful part in life and that she must give it its chance to show its merits; and for this purpose she seems to have chosen Leicester and Essex, who, though not intelligent men, were conspicuously masculine. Some of the most interesting passages in Professor Neale's *Elizabeth* contain his demonstrations that her dealings with both these nobles were very often just what one would have expected from an efficient monarch of either sex who was faced with imprudence and incompetence. One hates to say anything against Lytton Strachey in these days when he is insolently attacked by persons who are hardly fit to type his manuscripts; but it must be admitted that Professor Neale makes one doubt his view of Elizabeth in her relations with Essex as a demented semi-spinster incarnadined with sunset passions. It is more as if she hastily put back masculinity in its box and slammed the lid, seeing again that in her world it would not do.

This is indeed a most fascinating book, particularly in its disclosure of Elizabeth's financial genius and her steady pursuit of civilized ends. It shows us that if there is any peculiar grace about English life, we owe it to her, to the forty-five years she gave to the suppression of civil wars, the evasion of international dispute, the discouragement of torture by such ruses as giving prisoners money to escape. A complete pagan, she nevertheless had the religious hope that if one rooted up murder and riot out of life, it would develop a lovelier content. Her lies were curious prayers for England.